Just Rest

MELANIE REDD

Just Rest

No part of this work may be reproduced or transmitted in any form or by any means, electronic or mechanical, including photocopying and recording, or by any information storage or retrieval system, except as may be expressly permitted by the 1976 Copyright Act or in writing from the publisher. Requests for permission can emailed to info@endgamepress.com.

End Game Press books may be purchased in bulk at special discounts for sales promotion, corporate gifts, ministry, fund-raising, or educational purposes. Special editions can also be created to specifications. For details, contact Special Sales Dept., End Game Press, P.O. Box 206, Nesbit, MS 38651 or info@endgamepress.com.

Visit our website at www.endgamepress.com.

Library of Congress Control Number: 2021950470

ISBN: 978-1-63797-020-1
eBook ISBN: 978-1-63797-031-7

Cover Design by Bruce Gore, Gore Studio Inc.
Interior Design by Typewriter Creative Co.

Printed in India
TP
10 9 8 7 6 5 4 3 2 1

Just Rest

MELANIE REDD

This book is dedicated to every young woman who wants to find real rest.

Life is full of many things, people, and situations that will try to steal your rest and sap your peace.

Anxiety, depression, fear, insecurity, doubt, and other challenges come against you in this life.

My prayer is that you will learn to find ultimate rest in one place alone—at the feet of the Lord Jesus Christ. He is our rest. He is our peace.

Introduction

His name is Koda.

He's a huge fur ball that weighs in at a whopping seventy pounds.

Full of energy, always happy to see everyone, and cute as he can be, our three-year-old Australian shepherd fills our life with joy.

White, black, tan, and beige, he's a fully bred blue merle with one blue eye and one brown eye. We can't get enough of this dog.

However, he has one trait that detracts at times from his cuteness. Koda is a nervous and worrisome dog. He often has full-blown anxiety attacks and cannot be consoled during these times. Whether it's bad weather or a large truck passing by the house that causes him the anxiety, he can go into full panic mode and desperately searches for a place to hide.

Often, when Koda is the most upset, he will look for me.

Most of the time, he ends up on me, near me, or under me. Fear drives this animal to my side. To him, I'm the safest person in the world.

Why? It could be because I chose him at the groomer's house and held him in my arms for the entire four-hour journey to his new home. He may also behave in this manner because I'm the one who takes care of him, feeds him, fills his water bowl, and takes him for walks. My dog has

placed his complete trust in me because I have proven to be trustworthy.

Similarly, all of us have seasons when we are nervous and worried. Every human feels fear, doubt, and anxiety at times. Many people experience full-blown anxiety and panic attacks at times.

Whatever the case, we all find ourselves looking for a place to hide in certain moments. Fear drives us to look for safety, hope, and peace.

We need a trustworthy place where we can find rest for our souls.

That's what this book is all about.

Rest.

For your soul.

According to the Anxiety and Depression Association of America, anxiety and depression affect forty million adults in the US age 18 and above. This is 18 percent of the total population.[1]

I also read about a group of college counseling directors who were surveyed. Ninety-five percent of them said, "the number of students with significant psychological problems is a growing concern in their center or on campus."[2] In fact, this same article suggested that the biggest problem impacting college students today is anxiety. Depression was a close second.

It's possible that you are one of those students

who struggles with worry, fear, anxiety, or depression.

You could possibly deal with all these challenges. Or maybe you picked up this book because you would like to experience more rest, peace, and calmness deep within the depths of your soul. You are weary.

There is also a chance that your mom, grandmother, teacher, coach, or one of your mentors gave this book to you. You are reading it to be nice to them. That's okay too!

No matter your reason for reading, the goal is the same. We are going to learn how to find deep rest for your soul.

We will learn how to find peace in all aspects of life:

- Over worry
- Over anxiety
- When depressed or sad
- When bullied
- When your friends leave you out or don't understand you
- In your addictions
- In your health and finances
- When you feel stressed
- In your appearance
- As you choose your major
- As you decide your career
- For your future
- As you are dating or not dating
- When you feel alone
- When you lack inspiration

- As you feel homesick
- When there is FOMO
- When you feel competition
- As you deal with all the pressures of your life

I once read about a place that's deep below the ocean. It's called the "cushion of the sea."

Down beneath the surface that is agitated by storms, and driven about with winds, there is a part of the sea that is never stirred.

When we dredge the bottom and bring up the remains of animal and vegetable life, we find that they give evidence of not having been disturbed in the least, for hundreds and thousands of years.

The peace of God is that eternal calm which, like the cushion of the sea, lies far too deep down to be reached by any external trouble or disturbance; and he who enters into the presence of God, becomes partaker of that undisturbed and undisturbable calm.[3]

Quiet and peaceful no matter how loud the storms get.

That's what we are going for!

So, let's get started.

I'm praying you will experience the greatest peace and sweetest rest you have ever enjoyed.

Blessings,

What's in a Name?

When my mother was pregnant with me, she fell in love with the movie *Gone with the Wind*. This movie is based on a book, and both share a powerful story that is set in the Deep South during the American Civil War and Reconstruction era.

Two main female characters grace the silver stage: Scarlett and Melanie. When it came time to give me a name, my mom went with Melanie.

Growing up, I was the only Melanie I knew—at least for a long while. No one could pronounce or spell my name. I was often called Melissa, Melody, or Melinda. At times, I didn't really like the name I'd been given … until I found out what my name meant.

Turns out that my name means "relentless courage."

To be *Melanie* is to be an encourager.

And I am. God created me this way. My parents gave me my name. All of it fits perfectly together, just as our all-wise Creator knew it would.

Names matter.

Your name matters.

Your family name matters.

Your town name matters.

Your church name matters.

Your school or company name matters.

Even your street name matters.

Names are significant.

Names matter.

For that purpose, I've spent the last few months studying the names, the character, the meanings, and the promises behind the names of God.

Did you know that there are hundreds of names for God in the Bible?

We call him Lord, Shepherd, the Gardener, Almighty, Creator, and Father—just to list a few. From studying God's name, we can learn more about who He is and what He does. His names reveal more of His character and His ways.

Knowing the various names of God deepens our relationship with Him. It takes us to a new level of intimacy with our God.

For example, I'm mom, wife, friend, sister, aunt, pastor's wife, author, blogger, speaker, mentor, and coach. People get to know me by knowing these names. When I speak to groups of ladies, they get to know me as a teacher. But when we interact as friends at an event, they learn my heart and personality. Our relationships deepen.

The same is true for you.

As your co-workers, classmates, and neighbors see you around, they may know you from afar, in only one aspect of your character. But as they talk to you more and get to know you, they find out more about your personality, sense of humor, and compassion.

Our names are significant, just as God's names are significant.

Just Rest dives deep into the amazing names of God. As we discover more about who God is, I pray we will encounter Him personally as we never have before.

And as we encounter God in a greater way, we will begin to love Him even more. As we grow to love Him more, we will trust Him more. And as we trust Him more, we will find peace and calm, even when chaos surrounds us.

This is where the real rest begins—snuggled up close to the Lord.

Are you ready to *Just Rest?*

How to Use This Book

Welcome to Just Rest.

I am so grateful that you have picked up this book and joined us for this journey.

We have designed this resource with many features that we hope will add to your personal encouragement and devotional times. There are many thoughtful questions, stories, anecdotes, lists, and personal examples provided to offer you opportunities to *just rest*.

Over the days and weeks ahead as you read, journal, and pray, it is my prayer you will be inspired. The Bible is an incredibly powerful book, and I believe you will experience much hope and joy as you spend daily time with the Lord.

This is an easy-to-use resource for the active adult woman to incorporate into her daily life. We have organized everything so that you might achieve maximum spiritual growth in a minimum amount of time.

Daily Verses – Each day begins with a few moments in the Scriptures. We carefully and prayerfully selected each Bible verse or passage for this book to encourage you.

Daily Devotions – Following the daily verses, you will find a short devotional thought to inspire you to interact with God's Word. These devotions will offer personal experiences, stories, lists, Bible truths, and examples of how you can apply the spiritual nugget to your life.

Daily Declaration – After reading the daily verses and devotions, you will be encouraged to make a daily declaration (out loud) to start your day. The spoken word is powerful. It is our hope that, as you speak and hear yourself declaring the truth, you will be greatly impacted.

Daily Prayer – Once you have made your daily declaration, it will then be time to pray. Each devotion invites you to say a brief prayer. Of course, you may customize these prayers and talk to God for as long as you need. These prayers are intended to help launch you into your prayer time.

Daily Action – At the completion of each devotional, you will have a time to reflect. During these moments, you will be invited to interact with the devotional, consider your own life, and apply the message. Some of these challenges will invite you to make lists. Others will lead you into a time of reflection. On certain days, you will be asked to dream, draw, or share your ideas. All of these actions will impact your life profoundly—if you will take them.

Ready to start? Turn the page and let's get going.

Where Do We Find Rest?

Daily Verse – *Are you tired? Worn out? Burned out on religion? Come to me. Get away with me and you'll recover your life. I'll show you how to take a real rest. Walk with me and work with me—watch how I do it. Learn the unforced rhythms of grace. I won't lay anything heavy or ill-fitting on you. Keep company with me and you'll learn to live freely and lightly.* —Matthew 11:28-30 (MSG)

Can you recall a time when you were enjoying a piece of music or a song on the radio, and then you noticed a pause in the music? The music was once loud and grand, and then it grew quiet. Orchestras do this. Choirs do this. Musicians are familiar with this pause. It's known as a "rest." It is an intentional break in the activity … a planned moment of silence. And it can be powerful.

Rest. It's a theme that's wound throughout the events and days of our lives. In kindergarten, we take mats to school so we can enjoy rest time. When we travel, we make pit stops at roadside venues known as "Rest Stops." In sports, there is time-out given for teams to rest and regroup. And for most of us, we take time to rest each night for seven to eight hours.

Our souls need rest as well. We need time to be recovered, renewed, restored, refreshed, and replenished deep within our spirits. How can we accomplish this? Where do we find soul rest? Matthew teaches us that we experience real rest when we spend quality time in the presence of Jesus. Keeping company with Him causes us to live with a lighter load.

Do you need rest today? Press in close to Jesus. He is your place of ultimate rest.

Daily Declaration – *I declare that God is my safe place. When I am tired and burned out, I will go to Jesus. I will get away with Him and recover my life. He will show me how to take a real rest. I will walk with God, learn from God, and begin to live with a lighter load. As I spend time with Jesus, my life will be transformed.*

Daily Prayer – *Jesus, I need you today. I want to experience real rest in the depths of my soul. As I spend time with you, will you pour out your grace, hope, peace, and joy over my life? Thank you for showing me what it really means to rest in you.*

Daily Action – As you think about what rest looks like in your own life, how are you doing? Have your daily times with Jesus added much-needed rest to your world? What are two or three ways you can intentionally walk closer with Jesus today? For example, you could start a prayer journal, turn on Christian music, and take time to read one chapter in the Bible.

....

....

....

....

....

....

....

....

....

....

....

I've Had Enough!

Daily Verse – *Elijah was afraid and fled for his life. He went to Beersheba, a town in Judah, and he left his servant there. Then he went on alone into the wilderness, traveling all day. He sat down under a solitary broom tree and prayed that he might die. "I have had enough, LORD," he said. "Take my life, for I am no better than my ancestors who have already died."* —1 Kings 19:3-4 (NLT)

Do you ever feel like you have simply had enough? Most of us reach that point eventually—especially while in college and trying to get our lives and careers established. I have spoken with several young women who were constantly weary, stressed out, and overwhelmed. Maybe you can relate. If so, what should we do when we have had enough? Where do we turn?

In the verses above, Elijah had reached this point of breakdown in his life. *Enough was enough!* In the middle of the wilderness, he had an amazing moment alone with God while he was underneath a solitary broom tree. There are a few lessons we can learn from his experience.

- We all grow tired and want to quit at times. It is normal and part of life.
- Times of rest are needed and necessary.
- Without rest, we will burn out. Rest restores our souls.
- God knows what is coming next in our lives, and He will use these times of rest to prepare us.
- When it's time for us to get up and move again, God will send us back out to serve and work again.

Daily Declaration – *I declare that I am not able to go non-stop without rest. God has made me to come apart and be refreshed at times. I will be more in tune with my need to rest so that I will not burn out.*

Daily Prayer – *Father, would you help me become aware of when I push myself too hard? Would you give me grace with myself so that I can take a break, pause a moment, and receive refreshment? I ask for you to restore my soul, my body, and my mind. I need you.*

Daily Action – In our society today, the pressures are real. Do you feel them? Why not take a moment to carve out a time to rest? Where will you go? What will you do? (Consider taking a long walk, take a nap, or journaling.) How do you think this quiet time of rest will restore your soul and benefit your life?

The Pathway to Rest

Daily Verse – *This is what the LORD says: 'Stand at the crossroads and look; ask for the ancient paths, ask where the good way is, and walk in it, and you will find rest for your souls. But you said, "We will not walk in it."* —Jeremiah 6:16 (NIV)

If you came to my house for a visit, you'd have decisions to make, because there are several paths to my front door. You could take the sidewalk near the driveway or cut across the grass. There is also a cobblestone pathway leading from the mailbox. Any of these paths would grant you access to the front door, but the only one that is both fast and dry is the cobblestone pathway.

Similarly, in our spiritual lives, we can obtain real rest through various forms. But not all "pathways" are efficient. To find rest, we can get our nails done, enjoy a massage, take a nap, soak in the tub, or partake in several other self-care routines.

True rest for the soul, however, comes from one place only—and that involves walking in *the good way*. This is the path we choose when we walk close to Jesus. The pathway to rest is found in Him alone.

Daily Declaration – *I declare that God provides real rest. I will stand at the crossroads and look for the good way. I will walk in this way and stay as close to Jesus as I possibly can. By pressing in close to His side, I will find rest for my soul.*

Daily Prayer – *God, I want to walk close to you. Will you strengthen me to choose the pathway to rest every day? Thank you!*

Daily Action – What pathway do you typically take? The shortest one? The easiest one? The one that's right in front of you? How do you satisfy your desire to rest? Write about this in the space below.

Speaking Peace over Your Life

Daily Verse – *Jesus was in the stern, sleeping on a cushion. The disciples woke him and said to him, "Teacher, don't you care if we drown?" He got up, rebuked the wind and said to the waves, "Quiet! Be still!" Then the wind died down and it was completely calm.* —Mark 4:38-39 (NIV)

I'm sure you're familiar with the sounds of a loud thunderstorm. The winds howl. The rain pours. Lightning strikes as thunder rolls. Storms are noisy and often disconcerting. Soon, though, the storm passes, and a certain quiet descends. We often refer to this stillness as *the calm after the storm.*

As the disciples traveled with Jesus in a boat across a lake, a storm began to brew. Meanwhile, Jesus slept soundly in the bottom of the boat.

His disciples awoke him in sheer panic. Jesus, in his typical soothing manner, spoke to the wind—and everything grew still. The storm dissipated. Only peace remained.

Perhaps you find yourself in a storm today. Something has blown into your life and is now wreaking havoc upon you. Why not invite Jesus to speak peace over this issue? If He is able to handle the weather, don't you know He can handle your situation as well?

Daily Declaration – *I declare that God has the power to calm every storm. He is bigger than the chaos in my life. I trust Him to calm these situations and speak peace over them right now, in Jesus' name.*

Daily Prayer – *Lord, thank you for your great power and might. Thank you for quieting the winds and waves in my little world. Please take my situation(s) and speak peace over it today. I need your awesome touch in my life, God.*

Daily Action – In the space below, write about whatever troubles you. Is there a relationship, a job situation, a class issue, or a money problem you're currently facing? Or perhaps someone or something else is stealing your peace today. If so, take a few minutes to journal about it. Then, pray over this and ask God to calm your storm(s).

In the Nick of Time

Daily Verse – *Abraham looked up and there in a thicket he saw a ram caught by its horns. He went over and took the ram and sacrificed it as a burnt offering instead of his son. So Abraham called that place The LORD Will Provide. And to this day it is said, "On the mountain of the LORD it will be provided."* —Genesis 22:13-14 (NIV)

Want to know something interesting? Since we are familiar with the Old Testament stories such as this one, in a way, we get to cheat. How? Because when we read the story of Abraham and Isaac, we already know the ending. God provides! He provided a ram for them. But when Abraham was in the heat of the moment, he had no idea if God would, in fact, provide for them. His job was simply to remain obedient to God. God's job was to take care of everything else.

Abraham then gave this location—the area in which God provided for them—a relevant name. He called it, *"The LORD Will Provide."* The Hebrew name given here is Jehovah Jireh, meaning God sees and God provides.

Can I share something encouraging with you today? God sees your needs, and He wants to provide for you. So, what is it that you need right now? A friend? Forgiveness? Healing? Money? Hope? Rest assured, God sees your need, and He wants to be Jehovah Jireh in your life today.

Daily Declaration – *I declare that God is Jehovah Jireh, my Provider. He is well able to provide all that I need for my life, school, relationships, godly living, emotional support, and financial needs. I will trust in God today!*

Daily Prayer – *Would you give me the grace to trust in you to take care of me? Grow my faith, Lord. Help my unbelief. I desire to be a person who trusts you to provide for all my needs.*

Daily Action – How do you need God to be Jehovah Jireh in your life today? What are your current needs? Jot them down below, and then discuss each one of them with the Lord.

....

....

....

....

....

....

....

....

....

....

....

....

....

....

When We Need Him Most

Daily Verse – *We all experience times of testing, which is normal for every human being. But God will be faithful to you. He will screen and filter the severity, nature, and timing of every test or trial you face so that you can bear it. And each test is an opportunity to trust him more, for along with every trial God has provided for you a way of escape that will bring you out of it victoriously.* —1 Corinthians 10:13 (TPT)

When you were a child, did you ever do something that made you want to hide from your parents? I once played with matches as a kid, even after I was told not to, and I ended up burning one of my fingers. It hurt so much, but I didn't tell my parents because I didn't want to admit my wrongdoing. I was embarrassed and in pain—yet I had to deal with it all by myself.

In life, we are going to be tempted, tested, and drawn into all sorts of messes and dramas. We make dozens of choices each day. Could I suggest something that may seem counterintuitive? In the midst of facing our biggest temptations, let's run to Jesus. When you are the most tempted to sin, to blow it, or to do something stupid, stop for a moment and talk it over with the Lord. Why? Because He is the only One who promises an escape route.

Rather than running away from Him while facing a temptation, God wants us to run toward Him. Even during those times when we badly mess up, God gently whispers to us, "Come to Me, child." We do not need to face life's tests and temptations by ourselves. We have a Provider, a God who adores us and invites us to draw close to Him—even, and *especially*, in our messes and mishaps.

Daily Declaration – *I declare that God provides for me even while I face temptations. I can run to Him with my tests, trials, and temptations. I can press in close to Him even after I have made huge mistakes. He understands my pain and frustrations, and He loves me regardless.*

Daily Prayer – *Father, I want to learn to bring everything to you—the good, the ugly, the embarrassing, and the hurtful. I can trust you and talk to you about everything in my life. You will not turn away or abandon me, no matter how much I mess up.*

Daily Action – If we were to sit down over a cup of coffee today, what would you share with me? What is testing you right now? What tempts you the most? Take a few minutes to write about these things in the space below. Make a note of what you need most from God right now.

Holding Out on You

Daily Verse – For the Lord God is brighter than the brilliance of a sunrise! Wrapping himself around me like a shield, he is so generous with his gifts of grace and glory. Those who walk along his paths with integrity will never lack one thing they need, for he provides it all! —Psalm 84:11 (TPT)

Once, a group of my friends collected gifts, clothes, food, and household items for a missionary family who was returning to the states. All of us donated wonderful gifts and money to this family who had given up everything to follow Christ into full-time ministry. Everyone, that is, except one lady. Being blessed with great wealth, this lady had the most to give—and yet she gave the least.

Why is it that this happens so often? Out of stinginess, people hold back on what they give. But this is never the behavior of our God. He is generous and extends His gifts freely to us. He never holds back. Generosity and goodness define who God is!

How can we get in on His great provision? By walking close and enjoying our relationship with Him.

Can I tell you something amazing? God wants to wrap His presence around you like a shield and generously provide all you need for life and godliness. He wants to amaze you with His goodness today!

Daily Declaration – I declare that I serve a good God. I declare that God will wrap His presence around me like a shield and generously give me the gifts of His grace and glory. I will stay close to Him so that I will not miss a thing. I believe my God will provide for me.

Daily Prayer – Lord, thank you for your constant goodness in my life. Thank you for never holding out on your children. Thank you for your generosity and grace. I love you, Lord.

Daily Action – Do you ever feel like God is holding out on you? Why or why not? One way to overcome doubts and build faith is to thank God for His past kindness and goodness toward us. In the space below, write down eight to ten ways God has provided for you in the past, and then thank Him for these.

All of Your Needs

Daily Verse – *And my God will meet all your needs according to the riches of his glory in Christ Jesus.* —Philippians 4:19 (NIV)

It was unbelievable, really. Elizabeth, a friend of a friend, quit her job to be home with the kids while they were babies. But it wasn't the best of timing: the same week she quit her job, her husband lost *his* job. They suddenly had a huge house and no income. And the utility bill was due. They didn't tell anyone; instead, they prayed. Around the same time, our Bible study group was encouraged to take an offering for this family. We didn't even know them, but someone in the group had mentioned a need.

The money was collected and totaled to be $357. We inserted the money into an envelope and dropped it in the family's mailbox. Little did we know, earlier that day the wife had been kneeling on her kitchen floor, pleading with God to provide for the utility bill. What was the sum of her unpaid bill? $357! God had provided exactly what this family needed, and just in the nick of time.

The same God who met this young family's needs can meet your needs as well. So what do you need Him to do for you right now?

Daily Declaration – *I declare that God can meet all of my needs. He will take care of me. Today, I am trusting God's power to provide from His riches in glory in Christ Jesus.*

Daily Prayer – *Lord, I know you can supply my every need. Thank you for being the God who specifically takes care of His children. Thank you, in advance, for meeting every genuine need I have.*

Daily Action – In John 14:14, NIV, Jesus told us, "You may ask me for anything in my name, and I will do it." Perhaps today would be a good day for you to ask specifically for what you need. Take a few minutes and write down your greatest needs in the space below. Then, talk to God about these needs.

....

....

....

....

....

....

....

....

....

....

....

....

....

Tell God About Everything

Daily Verse – *Don't worry about anything; instead, pray about everything. Tell God what you need and thank him for all he has done. Then you will experience God's peace, which exceeds anything we can understand. His peace will guard your hearts and minds as you live in Christ Jesus.* —Philippians 4:6-7 (NLT)

It was a beautiful, breezy spring evening, and a group of ladies from an area church gathered across the church lawn to discuss the topic of finding hope. Uplifting worship music played. Food was provided. My church family enjoyed a sweet sense of community and a brief time of fellowship centered on God's Word. That evening, I took the stage to share encouraging reminders with those moms, daughters, and grandmothers. Perhaps these reminders can encourage you today as well.

1. Don't worry about anything. Worry does not accomplish anything good or productive.
2. Pray about everything. Literally talk to God about all things, all the time.
3. Be specific when you pray. Tell God what you want Him to do in your life. When you pray in a detailed manner, you will be clearer concerning the specific answers you need.
4. Be thankful when you pray. Thank God for what He has done and what He is about to do.
5. Present your cares before God, and then receive and experience His peace. This is what guards our hearts and minds and gives us hope.

The big question is: are you worrying or are you praying? It's really difficult (impossible, even) to do both at the same time!

Daily Declaration – *I declare that I can trust God completely. He is faithful, and He will take care of me. Because of this truth, I will pray about everything. When I talk over every issue with God, I will experience His incredible peace.*

Daily Prayer – *Father, I want to become a person whose life is saturated in prayer and thankfulness. You are the One who takes care of me. Help me to trust You and talk to You as I never have before.*

Daily Action – Since we are talking about prayer today, it seems like a great time to pray. I invite you to try this ACTS method of prayer: Adoration, Confession, Thanksgiving, and Supplication. Start with praise. Move to confession. Take time to be grateful. Then, pray over your heart's concerns. Use the space below to write out your prayer.

Where Do You Go First?

Daily Verse – *Seek the Kingdom of God above all else, and live righteously, and he will give you everything you need.* —Matthew 6:33 (NLT)

I went to college with a girl named Cathy. She lived a couple doors down from my roommates and me in our dorm during freshman year. She was funny, loud, outspoken, and full of life, and everyone loved her. She loved to seek out the counsel of her friends often. Regularly, she talked over her issues, decisions, and life problems with the girls who were on our section of the sixth floor.

What about you? Where do you go when you have issues or challenges? Who do you talk to? A friend, your boyfriend, your parents, or a mentor? As great as it can be to receive counsel from others, the Bible instructs us to seek God and His counsel for our lives first and foremost. We are to confide in Him before anyone else.

When we seek God and the things that matter to Him, He promises to take care of us. He is really the only One who has the power to do anything about most of our issues. Father God is able to meet our needs, and that is why we must turn to Him first.

Daily Declaration – *I declare that I will seek God for counsel before anyone else. He is my Provider. He is my Counselor. God is the main person who can solve or resolve my dilemma.*

Daily Prayer – *God, you are well able to meet the needs of my life. I will turn to you first and foremost. Only after that will I seek the counsel of my friends and family. Remind me to seek you first. Bolster my faith and trust in you.*

Daily Action – Think about my friend Cathy from college. Are you like her? Do you go to everyone with your problems before you talk to God? Why not change the order of things this week? I challenge you to talk to God first, and then talk to your friends and family. How might this make your life better? Different? Write about this below.

You Have Direct Access

Daily Verse – *Let us then approach God's throne of grace with confidence, so that we may receive mercy and find grace to help us in our time of need.* —Hebrews 4:16 (NIV)

During the first semester of my freshman year at Baylor University, I lost my favorite watch. This was long before the days of sports watches. My watch was silver, somewhat dainty, and fit my left wrist perfectly. I loved that watch.

Despite how long my friends and I searched, we simply could not locate the watch. So, I headed off to Bible class rather disappointed. My Bible professor, noticing my disappointment, invited me to her office after class so we could talk. When I told her about my lost watch, she did the most unbelievable thing. She unlatched the watch she wore on her left arm and handed it to me. "Until you get a new one," she said, "you can borrow mine." I was blown away at this gesture!

My Bible professor had invited me into her office and extended grace toward me. In a similar fashion, we are also invited into the presence of Almighty God where we can receive undeserved blessings. We can approach His throne of grace with confidence, knowing we will receive mercy and grace in our times of need. Lost watches, lost relationships, lost hope, lost confidence, and any other losses we face can be restored in His presence.

Daily Declaration – *As God's daughter, I can boldly approach His throne of grace. He adores me, loves to take care of me, and offers incredible mercy and grace toward me—especially in times of need.*

Daily Prayer – *Lord, sometimes I forget to approach your throne to ask for help. Thank you that you are always available and full of grace. When I am at a loss or in need, would you give me the courage to enter your presence?*

Daily Action – Perhaps you have never lost a watch before, but there is a good chance that you have suffered another kind of loss. What are two or three losses you have faced within the past year? Do you need to talk about any of these issues with God? Consider writing a prayer to God in the space below.

God Gives Freely

Daily Verse – *So, what do you think? With God on our side like this, how can we lose? If God didn't hesitate to put everything on the line for us, embracing our condition and exposing himself to the worst by sending his own Son, is there anything else he wouldn't gladly and freely do for us?* —Romans 8:31-32 (MSG)

I once heard preacher tell a fiction story that has stuck with me for years: An engineer spent his days overseeing a drawbridge that allowed trains to pass over a large river. Once the train would pass, the engineer maneuvered the gears to lift the drawbridge sides, allowing large boats to pass beneath.

On one particular day, the engineer's young son went to work with him. In the busyness of the workday, the man lost sight of his son. Just as he was reaching to lower the bridge so a train could pass, he saw his son playing below where the gears were located. That wasn't good, because if the bridge was to be lowered, allowing the train to pass, his son would be crushed.

You can imagine how conflicted the engineer must have been in that short moment of decision! But he didn't have much time to debate. He knew if the bridge was left up, the train—which was filled with people—would crash into the river.

The engineer chose to sacrifice his son in order to save those on the train. The passengers were never even aware of the sacrifice that was made for them that day.

That's what God did for us. He sent Jesus to die so that we might live. And if God would give us His Son, is there anything else he would withhold from us? God adores you. He placed everything on the line for you. Therefore, you can trust Him with everything in your life. Yes, everything!

Daily Declaration – *God is on my side; I cannot lose. He didn't hesitate to put everything on the line for me, embracing me even while I was still a sinner. Since He sent Jesus to die for me, I can also trust Him to completely take care of everything else.*

Daily Prayer – *Thank you, Lord, for loving me so much that you sent Jesus to die for me. I'm so grateful for the amazing love you have for me. Help me to trust you like I never have before.*

Daily Action – Most young women that I talk to understand that God send Jesus to die for them. But what does that look like in their daily lives? How does that knowledge increase their faith? How does it encourage your faith? Journal your ideas in the space below.

God Will Take Care of You

Daily Verse – *Take the carefree birds as your example. Do you ever see them worry? They neither grow their own food nor put it in a storehouse for later. Yet God takes care of every one of them, feeding each of them out of the abundance of his love and goodness. Isn't your life more precious to God than a bird? Be carefree in the care of God! Does worry add anything to your life? Can it add one more year, or even one day? So, if worrying adds nothing, but actually subtracts from your life, why would you worry about God's care of you?* —Luke 12:24-26 (TPT)

I come from a long line of great worriers. (Yes, worriers. Not warriors. Big difference.) Several of my ancestors are known for doing some professional level, grade A worrying. But as comedian Erma Bombeck once said, "Worry is like a rocking chair: it gives you something to do but never gets you anywhere."[4]

Maybe you are proficient at worrying as well. Perhaps you can whip yourself into a frenzy over what may happen or what could happen. *What about this job? What about that boy? What about my parents? What will my friends think? How am I going to get through this?*

But worry is not from God. In fact, today's verses remind us that God takes care of the birds. And if He can take care of the birds, how much more concerned is He about you? You matter to God; therefore, you can talk to Him about your issues, hurts, and worries. In the end, worry doesn't add anything profitable to our lives. It only subtracts from it. So why should we worry?

Daily Declaration – *I declare that God will take care of me. He cares for the birds in the air, and I matter to Him far more than they do. I don't have to worry because my God is Almighty and able to abundantly send me His love and goodness.*

Daily Prayer – *Thank you, Lord, for taking care of me and the things that matter to me. Thank you for your abundance and goodness in my life. I want to worry less and trust you more!*

Daily Action – Honesty time: Are you a worrier? If so, what tends to worry you the most? Try talking to God about your worries and your habit of worrying. And if you are not a worrier, take this time to thank God for the abundance He provides for you. God is always good to us.

....

....

....

....

....

....

....

....

....

....

....

....

Would You Like More Power?

Daily Verse – *Never doubt God's mighty power to work in you and accomplish all this. He will achieve infinitely more than your greatest request, your most unbelievable dream, and exceed your wildest imagination! He will outdo them all, for his miraculous power constantly energizes you.* —Ephesians 3:20 (TPT)

Do you like to eat sandwiches? Maybe a grilled cheese sandwich? If you're like me, maybe you prefer a sub sandwich that has tons of fun toppings. One of my favorite sandwiches is the Unwich from Jimmy John's. It's a lettuce wrap filled with my favorite sandwich ingredients, including bacon, tomato, lettuce, and avocado.

Today's verse is one I like to call the "The Power Sandwich." There are wonderful ingredients sandwiched between God's mighty power and His miraculous power. We are told that God will achieve infinitely more than…

- Your greatest request
- Your most unbelievable dream
- Your wildest expectation

Almighty God can outperform all of these things. How? Because of His power at work in our lives. Therefore, we must ask Him to show up in our lives. Let us learn how to pray, plan, dream, and think in such a way that God's power *must* show up to accomplish all of these things.

Daily Declaration – *I declare that God is able to accomplish much more than my greatest prayer requests. He can outdo my most unbelievable dreams and wildest expectations. I will start asking Him to do these things and trust that He will.*

Daily Prayer – *Wow, God—you are so awesome! I forget this sometimes. You are able to do exceedingly abundantly beyond all that I can ask or think. Beginning today, I want to experience this with you.*

Daily Action – Let's dream today! In the space below, write ten to fifteen amazing things you'd like to see come to pass in your life. These can be goals, plans, accomplishments, and anything that matters to you. Don't be afraid to make them big, scary, and daunting! Then, pray over each one and invite God to powerfully show up and blow you away.

Perfect Peace

Daily Verse – *You will keep in perfect peace all who trust in you, all whose thoughts are fixed on you! Trust in the LORD always, for the LORD GOD is the eternal Rock.* —Isaiah 26:3-4 (NLT)

Several years ago, my husband encouraged me to start golfing. For the most part, I really enjoy it … the time outdoors, the beautiful scenery, the opportunity to play with friends. But even though it's fun, it can be frustrating, too, primarily because of how challenging it is. My biggest challenge is learning how to relax and fix my eyes on the ball.

It's only when I focus on the ball, blocking out other distractions, that I can hit the ball pretty well. However, when I allow myself to become distracted by the other players, my nerves, squirrels and birds, or anything else, my golf game doesn't go so well. I *whiff* the ball or hit an errant shot.

In today's verses, we are told that we can have perfect peace. How? By trusting God, keeping our thoughts intentionally and purposely fixed on Him. But this can be hard. Distractions, people, and issues beg for our attention. Often, we allow our thoughts to wander and end up losing our peace. The secret to peace is to relentlessly refocus our attention back on God.

Daily Declaration – *I declare that God is my place of peace. By staying focused and concentrated on Him, I can have perfect peace. I trust God; He is my Eternal Rock. He is my Lord and Savior.*

Daily Prayer – *Father, it's easy to get distracted. Would you give me a greater ability to focus on you? Would you increase my capacity to trust you and bring perfect peace into my life?*

Daily Action – Most of us deal with distractions. All. Day. Long. What keeps you from peace? Who or what distracts you from focusing on the Lord? Write four to five of these distractions in the space below. Then go back and record one way you can fight against or overcome each distraction.

Ever Get a Song Stuck in Your Head?

Daily Verse – *Yes, indeed—God is my salvation. I trust, I won't be afraid. GOD—yes GOD!—is my strength and song, best of all, my salvation!* —Isaiah 12:2 (MSG)

Does a song get stuck in your head sometimes? Maybe a tune just seems to follow you around? Every time you turn on the radio or put in your earbuds, there it is. Many times, this type of tune will become *our song*—our go-to listen for a season.

I have one of these right now. I heard it a couple of months ago while I was folding towels. The first time I heard it, I was drawn in immediately. The words, the melody, the voices … I just love this song. Every time I hear it, I am encouraged. It's called *Jireh*, and it's written and performed by Maverick City Music and Elevation Worship. Maybe you've heard of it too.

One of the fun promises of the Bible is found in this verse today. Isaiah tells us that God is his salvation, strength, and song. What does that mean? Our God breathes music, words of hope, life, joy, and singing into our lives. He is your song, the tune of strength that needs to get stuck in your head. You don't have to be afraid because God is your strength, God is your song, and God is your salvation!

Daily Declaration – *I declare that I have hope today because of God. He is my salvation, and I will trust Him. I will not be afraid because God is my strength and my song. As He breathes His music into my soul, I will experience hope.*

Daily Prayer – *Lord, would you infuse hope into my life and become my song today? When I become scared, anxious, or afraid, would you remind me that you are strong, you are my strength, and you are able to save me?*

Daily Action – Let's talk music. What are your three favorite songs right now? Which one encourages you the most? Write these lyrics in the space below. Then, go throughout your day thinking about this song. Play it. Enjoy it. And let the lyrics bring you hope.

Overwhelmed, in a Good Way

Daily Verse – *Yes, God is more than ready to overwhelm you with every form of grace, so that you will have more than enough of everything—every moment and in every way. He will make you overflow with abundance in every good thing you do.* —2 Corinthians 9:8 (TPT)

Have you ever been overwhelmed—in a good way? Perhaps you have been blown away by the kindness of God or that of another person. Maybe a worship service has brought you to tears or to your knees at one time. Have you seen God do a miracle that you never imagined could happen, or have you experienced the answer to a long-awaited prayer? This is evidence of the overwhelming, unbelievable grace of God.

Grace is one of my favorite words in the Bible. It implies that we gain something we didn't work for and don't really deserve. It's a gift. And Scripture tells us that God is more than ready to overwhelm us with every form of grace. He wants us to have more than enough of everything. Our God desires for us to overflow with abundance in everything that we do.

What does this look like? Picture the most beautiful fountain you have ever seen, overflowing with water from top to bottom. That's what God wants for your life. He wants you to be flowing from head to toe with wisdom, joy, hope, and abundance. God wants you to be a mighty woman, able to handle everything that life throws at you today. Overwhelmed with grace. More than enough. Pouring out hope and abundance.

Daily Declaration – *I declare that God wants to overwhelm me with grace today. I declare that I will have more than enough of everything for every moment and in every way. God will make me overflow with abundance in every good thing I do.*

Daily Prayer – *Father, would you make me a beautiful fountain of grace to everyone around me? I want to overflow as I am overwhelmed by your goodness. Thank you that I am enough because you are enough. Strengthen my resolve and my faith in your power to provide. I want to trust you more than I ever have to take care of what concerns me.*

Daily Action – What has overwhelmed you in a good way lately? Have you seen God at work? Experienced a miracle? Been blown away by grace? If so, share your experience below. If not, this is a great time for you to invite God to blow you away with His goodness and grace. Write your prayer below.

Under His Wings

Daily Verse – *He will cover you with his feathers, and under his wings you will find refuge; his faithfulness will be your shield and rampart. You will not fear the terror of night, nor the arrow that flies by day, nor the pestilence that stalks in the darkness, nor the plague that destroys at midday.* — Psalm 91:4-6 (NIV)

Years ago, I read the story about a massive fire that had swept through Yellowstone National Park. This fire destroyed a large portion of the park and harmed many of the trees and park animals. Once the fire had been extinguished, the firefighters conducted search, rescue, and cleanup efforts and discovered an amazing sight.

Amid the rubble and charred remains, the chirping of little birds caught their attention. As they lifted the lifeless body of a mother bird from the ground, they found several healthy, happy little baby birds—unharmed and full of life. The mother bird had sacrificed her life to save and shelter those precious baby birds beneath her wings.

Did you know that God is compared to a large bird in the Bible? We are told that we are covered by His feathers and kept safe underneath His wings. Because of his protection, you don't have to be afraid of anything. Not darkness. Not disease. Not chaos. Not even other people. We don't need to fear anyone or anything. Instead, let's press in close to the Lord and live safely beneath those powerful wings. He is our Shield, our Rescuer, and our Safe Place.

Daily Declaration – *I declare that I have a God who protects me. As I remain underneath His wings, He provides safety, security, and peace. I declare that my God is strong, powerful, and able to take care of me. I am safe in His care.*

Daily Prayer – *Lord, this world is crazy, and I need to remember to dwell in the safety of your wings. Remind me to stay close to you. I want to live under your wings of protection and power.*

Daily Action – Why do you suppose the mother bird gave her life for those babies? Have you ever experienced God's protection? What has this been like for you? Going forward, what are two or three ways you can press in closer to God's wings of safety and protection?

God Has Great Things Ahead for Your Life

Daily Verse ⸱ *"For I know the plans I have for you," says the Lord. "They are plans for good and not for disaster, to give you a future and a hope."* —Jeremiah 29:11 (NIV)

When my husband was the missions pastor at a wonderful church in the Atlanta area, he was given the opportunity to travel all over the world. One of his travel companions was a senior saint who was in his eighties. This man had served in the US Military and fought in many wars, and he especially liked to visit countries where he had fought on behalf of the people's freedom.

When this older gentleman entered a place, he wore his military uniform and went to the town square or city center to meet everyone. These people were drawn to this man in uniform and would want to shake his hand and thank him for his service. They told him about how much they appreciated his sacrifice in fighting for their freedom. These conversations gave him multiple opportunities to share the gospel.

Likewise, God has amazing plans for your life. With His skilled hand, the Creator weaves your experiences, battles, challenges, and uniforms together for hope and with purpose. Author Jonathan Daugherty puts it this way, "God made your life to matter. You are not an accident; you have a significant purpose."

Daily Declaration – *I declare that God has great plans ahead for my life. His plans for me are for good and not for disaster. In Christ, I have a future and a hope. I am not an accident. I declare that God has made my life to accomplish significant purposes.*

Daily Prayer – *Father, would you help me to believe that you really do have a good purpose for my life? I sometimes don't see it, feel it, or believe it; however, it is still one of your promises. Encourage me to trust in your plans for my future.*

Daily Action – When you think about your future, what are you most looking forward to? What are two or three things you feel gifted, equipped, and called to do with your life? Write some of these purposes in the space below. Then, share them with a trusted friend or mentor.

God Sees

Daily Verse – *She answered GOD by name, praying to the God who spoke to her, "You're the God who sees me! "Yes! He saw me; and then I saw him!"* —Genesis 16:13 (MSG)

This woman did nothing wrong. In fact, she did everything she was commanded to do. When her boss instructed her to complete certain tasks, she obeyed without question, even when the requests seemed odd or even inappropriate.

On this day, however, things went a little too far, and the cruelty of her boss sent her packing. She fled off in tears, trying to grapple with the horrible situation she had found herself in. This lady's name was Hagar, and she was all alone, scared, hurt, and completely unsure of what to do next.

It was in this moment that the angel of the Lord showed up. He found her sitting alone by a stream, rejected and discouraged. The angel encouraged her, instructed her, and uplifted her. She felt like someone had really understood her pain. Hagar assigned a name to this place where the angel met with her: "The God Who Sees Me."

Did you know God sees you as well? He understands your pain. He hears your cries. He sees your tears. And He is aware of everything you are facing right now.

Daily Declaration – *I declare that my God is a God who sees me. He doesn't miss a thing. God is completely aware, in tune, and caught up on my situations at work, in school, with my family, and in my relationships. I believe that God is not a clueless deity. I declare that God is well-acquainted with every detail of my life.*

Daily Prayer – *Thank You for being the God who sees, hears, and notices. Nothing gets past you! I'm grateful to serve a God who cares about the hurts, needs, dramas, and issues of a young woman like me.*

Daily Action – If an angel of the Lord were to come to your apartment, dorm room, or car today, what would you want to discuss with Him? Write some of your biggest concerns below. Then, bring them to the God who sees and loves you greatly.

Details, Details, Details

Daily Verse – *You have searched me, LORD, and you know me. You know when I sit and when I rise; you perceive my thoughts from afar. You discern my going out and my lying down; you are familiar with all my ways. Before a word is on my tongue you, LORD, know it completely.* —Psalm 139:1-4 (NIV)

Are you a detail-oriented person—like the kind of girl who keeps a calendar on her phone? Do you prefer to have a plan, a schedule, and an agenda for everything? Most of us like to have at least some kind of plan over these details in our lives.

God is aware of both the huge things and the intricate details. On one hand, He oversees the universe, weather, past, present, and future. On the other hand, He is intimately involved in every detail of each of our lives. Isn't that mind-blowing?

For example, the Bible tells us that He knows when we sit down and when we stand up. Before we speak, He knows what we will say. God is aware of our thoughts, our emotions, our struggles, and the matters that weigh heavy on our hearts. Your God knows all about you, and He loves you more than you can imagine.

Daily Declaration – *I declare that God is interested and invested in the details of my life. He is not some distant deity who doesn't care. Rather, He is involved and aware of my life. He loves me and cares about everything that is happening in me and around me.*

Daily Prayer – *Thank you, Lord, that you are aware of what's going on in my little world. Even when no one else knows, asks, or seems concerned, thank you that you see, and you know. Thank you for caring about me and my everyday circumstances. Thank you for how much you love me.*

Daily Action – As you look at your agenda for the day, bring each item to God. Pray through your calendar, work schedule, class schedule, meetings, and whatever else you have going on. Then, think about two or three concerns you have today and write a prayer about each of these. Ask God for extra grace and wisdom in each of these matters.

His Eyes Are on Us

Daily Verse – *The eyes of the LORD search the whole earth in order to strengthen those whose hearts are fully committed to him. —2 Chronicles 16:9a (NLT)*

Her name was Mrs. Smith, and her daughter Kara was one of my best friends. When Kara and I were teenagers, we would sit away from our parents in church. But Mrs. Smith would always find us. And she would watch us like a hawk. Her gaze would be glued on us throughout the entire service. I wonder if Mrs. Smith even had a chance to enjoy the sermons during that time!

Much like Mrs. Smith, our God has his eyes on us. He sees. Nothing gets past His sight. In Proverbs 15:3, we read, "The eyes of the LORD are everywhere, keeping watch on the wicked and the good." No matter where we go, what time it is, or what is taking place, God sees it all.

What does this mean for us? The Bible tells us that God searches high and low to find people whose hearts are directed toward Him. He wants to strengthen us and fill us with hope and grace. As God's attention is on you today, what do you need Him to do in your life?

Daily Declaration – *I declare that God is the God who sees all things. His eyes are everywhere, and nothing gets past Him. He wants to strengthen and help me as I surrender my heart and life to Him.*

Daily Prayer – *Thank you, Lord, that I am never out of your sight. I'm grateful that you see everything and are aware of everything. Would you strengthen me and fill me with your hope and grace? I need you today!*

Daily Action – How does it feel knowing that God sees everything? Does it bother you, encourage you, or do you have mixed feelings about it? What are two or three ways you need God to strengthen and support you today? Jot these down in the space below and bring them to the Lord.

God is Watching Over You

Daily Verse – *The LORD watches over you—the LORD is your shade at your right hand; the sun will not harm you by day, nor the moon by night. The LORD will keep you from all harm—he will watch over your life; the LORD will watch over your coming and going both now and forevermore.* —Psalm 121:5-8 (NIV)

I attended college in Waco, Texas at Baylor University. When I visited home in Memphis, Tennessee during this time, I would either drive twelve hours or fly home. One year, as I drove to the airport in Dallas, it began to rain. Not just a little. It poured so much that I could barely see the road ahead.

Although I was in a hurry—after all, I had a flight to catch—I decided to pull beneath the covering of an overpass and wait for the rain to subside. (These were the days before we had cell phones.)

A man tapped my window. He asked if I was going to the airport like he was and suggested I could follow his car; that way, I could arrive safely. I took him up on the offer and arrived at the airport without an incident.

During this time, my parents—who were in Tennessee—were praying for my safety. We've always speculated that the man who offered help was my guardian angel.

Simply put: God watches over us. He is our keeper, our protector, and our guardian.

Daily Declaration – *I declare that my God watches over me. He is my shade, so the sun won't harm me. He keeps me from harm and watches over my life. I declare that God will take great care of me. I trust Him to protect me.*

Daily Prayer – *Thank you for your protection and care. Thank you for looking out for me and watching over me. I'm grateful that you are my protector, my guardian, and my keeper.*

Daily Action – Have you ever had an experience like mine where you enjoyed God's protection or help? What happened? How did you see God work? Write about it in the space below.

....

....

....

....

....

....

....

....

....

....

....

....

....

You Are His Masterpiece

Daily Verse – *For we are God's masterpiece. He has created us anew in Christ Jesus, so we can do the good things he planned for us long ago. —Ephesians 2:10 (NLT)*

A couple of years ago, my friend Beth experienced terrible back issues. She couldn't do anything but lay on the couch and pray. However, she believed that God still had a plan and a purpose for her life. Because of that, she asked God to use her despite her back issues.

People called and asked if they could visit her. They brought food and flowers, and then they poured out their hearts to her, crying as they shared. She listened, offered hope, and prayed for them. For months, Beth ministered to people like this while lying flat on her back—in pain, nonetheless!

If God can use Beth, then He can use you too! You may think it's too late or too hard. Or maybe you believe you've made too many mistakes, that you have nothing to offer, or that God has passed you over. None of these assumptions are true!

God is not finished with you yet. He is still accomplishing amazing things through His people and for His people.

My pastor, Adrian Rogers, says regularly, "If you woke up this morning, God still has a plan for your life!"

Daily Declaration – *I declare that I am God's masterpiece. He created me anew in Christ Jesus and has awesome things for me to accomplish. God has a great plan for my life, and He wants to use me to impact the world for good.*

Daily Prayer – *Thank you for designing me to make a difference in this world for your kingdom. You have wonderful plans for my life. You can still use me, no matter what my past looks like.*

Daily Action – As you look ahead toward the future, how would you like God to use you to make a difference? Who would you like to help? What problems would you like to help solve? Where do you want to invest your life? Jot a few ideas in the space below.

Generation After Generation

Daily Verse – *Know therefore that the LORD your God is God; he is the faithful God, keeping his covenant of love to a thousand generations of those who love him and keep his commandments.* —Deuteronomy 7:9 (NIV)

When I was born, each of my grandparents and great-grandparents were alive and well. I had the chance to meet them as a child. What about you? Have you been blessed to know your grandparents? Great-grandparents? Uncles, aunts, and cousins? If so, realize that you have enjoyed something special.

One way we can maintain steadfast trust in God is by reflecting on how He has cared for those who have come before us. As we remember how God provided for our parents or grandparents, we become encouraged. When we reflect on how God took care of a teacher, pastor, mentor, friend, or coach in our lives, we become uplifted.

Look for the threads of God's faithfulness in your own life. Remember the many ways He has shown His faithfulness toward you. Consider the evidence of His goodness in your own life. As you ponder how He has cared for you in the past, you will trust Him to be faithful in the future, and your faith will be boosted.

Daily Declaration – *I declare that the same God who cared for my parents and grandparents will care for me as well. God has brought me this far and He will not leave me now. My God will continue to be faithful. I trust in Him and in His love for me.*

Daily Prayer – *Father, you have been our help in the past, and I thank you that you will continue to provide. You have an amazing track record of taking care of your people. Help me to trust you to continue caring for me.*

Daily Action – Make a list of four or five ways God has provided for you over the past year. For example, maybe God sent a friend, financial help, emotional support, a gift, or something else that confirmed how much He cares for you. Write some of these past provisions and thank God for this evidence of His faithfulness.

....

....

....

....

....

....

....

....

....

....

....

....

....

....

Abounding in Love and Faithfulness

Daily Verse – *And he passed in front of Moses, proclaiming, "The LORD, the LORD, the compassionate and gracious God, slow to anger, abounding in love and faithfulness, maintaining love to thousands, and forgiving wickedness, rebellion and sin."* —Exodus 34:6-7a (NIV)

Growing up, my family lived in the same house and neighborhood, attended the same church, kept the same friends, and lived a consistent life. Few changes were made. After I attended college and got married, my husband, the kids, and I have moved many times, lived in several cities and attended multiple churches over the years, and enjoyed making friends across the United States. Life as an adult has been anything but the same.

How about you? Have you moved a lot? Attended more than one school? Found a faith family in more than one church? Made friends in more than one place? If so, you may totally understand how life changes. Things don't remain the same. Transition, starting over, moving, and relocating are a normal part of our lives.

But I have good news for you: despite the constant changes in life, God remains the same. He is consistently faithful, dependable, reliable, and trustworthy. When the rest of the world feels unsteady, we can rely on the God who supports and upholds us. During times when we feel unsteady, God is available to keep us steady.

Daily Declaration – *I declare that God is faithful. He is the steady foundation in my life—dependable, available, and always ready to hear my heart. I can depend on Him. I can lean on Him.*

Daily Prayer – *God, please remind me to look to you sooner and more often. You are reliable. I want to depend on you like I never have before. Thank you for being a faithful God throughout generations of believers.*

Daily Action – How has God proven His constant faithfulness in your life? How has He steadied you in the past? Take time to write out a prayer of praise, thanking God for His goodness and faithfulness.

....

....

....

....

....

....

....

....

....

....

....

....

Every Single Morning

Daily Verse – *The faithful love of the LORD never ends! His mercies never cease. Great is his faithfulness; his mercies begin afresh each morning.* —Lamentations 3:22-23 (NLT)

We are coffee lovers at our house. In fact, we just purchased a new espresso machine to go alongside our Keurig coffee maker. To make room for these machines, we also bought a wonderful coffee cart to store coffee cups, an assortment of coffee roasts, and other wonderful coffee-related supplies. (If you are not into coffee, you may not get all of this.)

Each morning, I wake up and have a fresh cup of coffee (or two). I have to have a fresh mug, coffee pod, and water. Coffee leftover from the day before just wouldn't cut it. I need it to be new every single morning.

Similarly, I love that we can receive God's mercies afresh every morning. We don't need to depend on yesterday's mercies. At the dawn of each new day, God offers us His faithful mercies. Each sunrise is an opportunity for us to look to God for hope and for help to survive another day.

Daily Declaration – *I declare that God's faithful love never ends! His mercies never cease. God is faithful and offers me His mercies afresh every morning. He is enough, and I am enough today.*

Daily Prayer – *Father, thank you for your faithfulness and mercy. I need it every day. Would you flood me with your mercies and grace today? I ask that you pour your love and goodness over my life.*

Daily Action – Are you a coffee drinker? If so, what coffee do you prefer? If not, what do you like to drink to help get you started in the morning? What do God's daily mercies look like for you? How have you experienced His faithfulness and goodness in your life? Consider journaling about this below.

You Can Turn to God

Daily Verse – *My salvation and my honor depend on God; he is my mighty rock, my refuge. Trust in him at all times, you people; pour out your hearts to him, for God is our refuge.* —Psalm 62:7-8 (NIV)

Have you ever felt lost? Alone? Uncertain? Wounded? Where do you turn during these times? Maybe you call a friend, go for a run, or hit the gym. Or maybe you prefer to turn to food, drinks, music, Netflix, or another mind-numbing activity.

Could I offer a suggestion? The next time you feel overwhelmed, run to God instead. Get alone with Him. Pour your heart out. He is your mighty rock, your refuge, and your safe place. When you aren't sure what else to do, turn to God.

Sometimes I have to go to my closet and sit on the floor. I'll lift my arms to heaven, look up, and cry out, "Help!" Every time I get alone with God like this, I am changed. Peace floods over me. A sense of calm fills me. A deep sense of hope returns. By running to God and spending a few moments alone with Him, I become completely transformed. The same can be true for you as well.

Daily Declaration – *I declare God is my refuge. I can run to Him for help. When I am struggling, I can pour out my heart to Him. My God is trustworthy. He wants me to come to Him and allow Him to transform me.*

Daily Prayer – *Thank you that you love spending time with me. When I have a hard day, rather than turning to everything and everyone else, I want to turn to you first.*

Daily Action – Where do you turn when you have a bad day? Who do you call? Do you turn to God? How are you helped by turning to God? What difference does He make in your life? Complete this sentence: If I turned to God more often, I think...

....

....

....

....

....

....

....

....

....

....

....

....

....

Where is Your Safe Place?

Daily Verse – *In the day of trouble, he will treasure me in his shelter, under the cover of his tent. He will lift me high upon a rock, out of reach from all my enemies who surround me. Triumphant now, I'll bring him my offerings of praise, singing and shouting with ecstatic joy! Yes, I will sing praises to Yahweh!* —Psalm 27:5-6 (TPT)

When I was in elementary school, my dad built my brother and me a wonderful playhouse on stilts in our backyard. It had a real roof on top and a trap door to keep us safe. Since I grew up in a neighborhood that contained mostly boys and several bullies, this house quickly became my safe place. My shelter. When I faced trouble with the other kids, I would run to this little house and bolt the trap door. I felt safe from the mean kids and threats that surrounded me.

Perhaps there are people or situations that cause you to feel unsafe, unsettled, or maybe even bullied. (If so, you may need to let someone know if things feel out of control or unhealthy.)

On days when life becomes too much, turn to God. He can be like your little house, your place to hide when the "neighborhood kids" chase and bother you. When you feel left out or misunderstood, allow Him to be your safe place—your constant place of refuge.

Daily Declaration – *I declare that God is my safe place. He is my shelter, my tent of safety. I can turn to Him and be saved from my enemies. I declare that God is my refuge.*

Daily Prayer – *Thank you, Lord, for being my little house, my place of safety. Remind me to turn to you when those around me make me feel unsafe. I praise you for being my refuge.*

Daily Action – We all need safe places to turn. What does this look like for you? Where do you feel most safe? Is it a certain location? Does God feel like a safe place for you to turn? Are there any ways you could allow Him to become a shelter for you? You may want to write about this in the space below.

No Peace Like Home

Daily Verse – *Lord, you have been our dwelling place throughout all generations. Before the mountains were born or you brought forth the whole world, from everlasting to everlasting you are God.* —Psalm 90:1-2 (NIV)

When you think about the word *home*, what comes to mind? A place? Feeling? Smell? Group of people? In the simplest terms, home is that place where we feel most ourselves. It's that space that welcomes us and gives us peace. From the moment we arrive home, our blood pressure drops, we get comfortable, and we feel most at ease.

Did you know God is a type of "home" for us? In the verses today, we read Moses's prayer. He calls God a "dwelling place throughout all generations." Our God is a refuge, sanctuary, hiding place, and stability for us. He invites us to draw close to Him and obtain peace in his presence.

What might this look like? For me, this requires that I intentionally take time each day to sit quietly at God's feet. I picture myself looking into His grace-filled eyes and talking with Him. When I press in close, I experience an incredible calmness. My blood pressure drops. I get comfortable. I feel more at ease. It's a practice that I encourage you to try as well!

Daily Declaration – *I declare that God is my home. He is my safe place, my dwelling place, and my sanctuary. As I press in close to Him, I will find calmness, hope, and peace.*

Daily Prayer – *Thank you for being our dwelling place. From the earliest Bible days, people have been drawing close to you and finding great peace. I'm grateful that I can enjoy you and your presence. You are my home.*

Daily Action – In the space below, draw or describe your home. What does it look like? What are some significant features? What do you love about it? Now, think about God as your home. What might this look like? How can you begin to draw closer to Him and enjoy more time in His presence?

Drama. Drama. Drama.

Daily Verse – *You hide them in the shelter of your presence, safe from those who conspire against them. You shelter them in your presence, far from accusing tongues.* —Psalm 31:20 (NLT)

Drama. *Drama. Drama.* Do you ever have drama with others in your life? Misunderstandings. Gossip. Rejection. Betrayal. Cruel words. Conspiracies. So much drama. All of us have been in the midst of it before; in fact, we may have ignited the drama ourselves at some time. Yet at other times, we may have just been in the wrong place, at the wrong time.

Whatever the case, we must often navigate the tricky and unpredictable steps through the dramatic moments of our lives. What do we say? How do we respond? Who should we talk to first? How do we fix this mess? I've discovered that it's in these moments when I need to escape into God's presence to receive clarity and the right perspective.

What might this look like for you?

- Walking outside to clear your head and pray.
- Listening to worship music.
- Sitting with the Lord and breathing deeply.
- Reading the Psalm.

Daily Declaration – *I declare that God is my shelter and my safe place in the middle of drama. When someone conspires against me, speaks against me, or hurts me, I will shelter in close to Him.*

Daily Prayer – *Thank you for being a safe shelter in the middle of crazy relationships and situations. I know I can always turn to you when I face the drama. Help me to remember this and to seek you often for help and wisdom.*

Daily Action – Can you think of the last drama you were involved in? What happened? How did you respond? How do you think it will help to start spending time with God during the dramas of life? How do you suppose God will make things better, less painful, and more peaceful? Share your ideas in the space below.

Cities of Refuge

Daily Verse – *"The eternal God is your refuge, and underneath are the everlasting arms. He will drive out your enemies before you, saying, 'Destroy them!'"* —Deuteronomy 33:27 (NIV)

During the Old Testament days, God orchestrated an interesting provision. When an accident occurred involving one person unintentionally killing another, the accidental killer was able to flee to a city of refuge until his case could be heard. The cities of refuge protected the person from retaliation from the victim's family.

For example, if two people were chopping down a tree and the tree fell off course, causing one of them to die, the other person could then flee to the city of refuge and present their case to the court. Similarly, we have places today that we deem "sanctuary cities." These cities protect undocumented immigrants when dealing with police.

In our lives, God is a city of refuge. He is our sanctuary city. We can run to Him for shelter no matter what we have done, how badly we have blown it, or how much we have messed up. His arms are open wide, and He stands ready to hear us and to protect us. Will we run to Him for safety today?

Daily Declaration – *I declare that the Lord is my city of refuge. I can always run to His arms. I declare that no matter what I have done, God will open His arms wide and hold me. I am safe with Him, in Him, and near Him.*

Daily Prayer – *Thank you, Father, that you are my sanctuary city. You are my refuge where I can run in the day of trouble. When I feel scared, threatened, misunderstood, nervous, or hurt, I can find shelter in you.*

Daily Action – Where do you tend to run when you're afraid? Do you go to a person, a substance, a habit, Netflix, bed, or to God? How might your life improve if you regularly ran to the Lord when you need help? How might things get better if you made him your city of refuge on a regular basis?

When Feeling Oppressed

Daily Verse – *The LORD is a refuge for the oppressed, a stronghold in times of trouble. Those who know your name trust in you, for you, LORD, have never forsaken those who seek you.* —Psalm 9:9-10 (NIV)

There is an off-the-grid retreat, known as "The Moriah House," that allows women and their children to escape, at no cost, when they are oppressed. Oppression may involve domestic violence, a difficult divorce, or a great loss that is tearing their life apart. For up to a year, these women can live without fear, be encouraged in God's Word while they are being housed and fed and find sweet relief in desperate times of trouble.

To be abused mentally or physically can cause us to become oppressed. We can also become oppressed when we suffer unjust treatment, face emotional distress, or become burnt out with life in general. It's possible you are experiencing oppression in your life today. You may be fighting depression or perhaps reeling from a breakup or abusive relationship.

If you, or a close friend, are facing oppression today, there is hope. God promises to serve as our refuge in times of trouble. We can trust in Him and lean on Him. Additionally, I encourage you to reach out for help. Call a counselor, a local Bible study teacher, or a mentor. Confide in them about the challenges you are facing. You don't have to go through this alone!

Daily Declaration – *I declare that God is greater than my oppression and stronger than my depression. I can take my hurts, frustrations, and sadness to Him. He is never offended. Instead, He invites me to lean on Him so that He can become my stronghold in times of trouble.*

Daily Prayer – *Father, I'm glad that you understand my emotions, my hurts, and my grief even more than I do. You not only "get" me, but you also love me more than I can imagine. I want to trust you completely with everything that weighs on my heart today.*

Daily Action – Even as Christian women, we can experience seasons of sadness, being overwhelmed, depression, and oppression. You may be in one of those seasons today. If so, consider writing an honest prayer to God about how you are feeling. And if you are doing well today, take time to pray for a friend or family member who could be struggling with oppression.

Those Crazy Headlines

Daily Verse – *God, you're such a safe and powerful place to find refuge! You're a proven help in time of trouble—more than enough and always available whenever I need you. So, we will never fear even if every structure of support were to crumble away. We will not fear even when the earth quakes and shakes, moving mountains and casting them into the sea. For the raging roar of stormy winds and crashing waves cannot erode our faith in you.* —Psalm 46:1-3 (TPT)

As soon as I awoke this morning, I checked my phone for messages and was greeted with a couple of texts, Instagram alerts, and other notifications. Then I noticed several breaking news headlines: hurricane in the Gulf, battles over free speech, shootings in Chicago, among other bad news. Maybe you get these notifications on your phone too.

It can be rather depressing to see these headlines and sometimes even alarming. My heart tends to beat faster when I see this, and fear creeps into my mind. But when I feel panic trying to grip me, I must remember that God is in all of this. Author Oswald Chambers puts it this way, "All our fret and worry is caused by calculating without God."[5]

God says that He is a safe and powerful place of refuge. He is our proven help in times of trouble. Our God is more than enough, and He is always available when we need Him. Even when structures of support crumble, He is our safe shelter. When the earth shakes and the waves crash, we can have faith in Almighty God.

Daily Declaration – *I declare that God is my refuge no matter what happens around me. When the world is chaotic and the storms come, I declare that I can completely trust God and depend on Him. I will not give in to fear or allow it to destroy my faith!*

Daily Prayer – *Sometimes, Lord, things feel so out of control. The news, the headlines, and the chaos become overwhelming. Would you steady my heart today, no matter how hard the winds of life blow?*

Daily Action – Honesty time. What causes you to fear the most? What ushers panic, worry, and doubt into your life? Make a list of seven or eight things that cause you the most anxiety today, then bring each one to the Lord.

....

....

....

....

....

....

....

....

....

....

....

....

God is Your Shield

Daily Verse – *After this, the word of the LORD came to Abram in a vision: "Do not be afraid, Abram. I am your shield, your very great reward." —*Genesis 15:1 (NIV)

Have you ever driven a vehicle that didn't have a windshield? Maybe it was a golf cart, a motorcycle, or even a bicycle. When our vehicle lacks a windshield, the wind can be harsh on our skin and eyes. And without protective glass, we must face the elements head on—such as increased temperatures and insects.

In the book of Genesis, God promises to be a shield to Abram. A shield serves as armor, protection, and is an absorber. A good shield not only protects from the front, but it also protects from the sides and the rear. Powerful shields work to guard on all sides. In Psalm 139:5, David puts it this way: "You have surrounded me on every side, behind me and before me, and You have placed Your hand gently on my shoulder." (TPT)

What does this mean for you? God is your shield as well. He hems you in on every side. His love surrounds, encircles, and protects you. As you face that class, exam, job, boss, boy, girl, or challenge, you can move forward, trusting that God surrounds you; He encloses you in His armor today.

Daily Declaration – *I declare that you are the shield of my life. Since you are for me, no one can stand against me. I will face this day with courage because you surround me on every side.*

Daily Prayer – *Thank you for being my shield. As you were faithful to protect Abram, you will be faithful to protect me. I lean on you and trust in you today.*

Daily Action – Does it encourage you to know that God surrounds you with protection? How have you experienced Him as a shield in your life? What do you need Him to buffer and shield you from today? Share about that need in the space below.

Victory Over Your Enemies

Daily Verse – *"How blessed you are, O Israel! Who else is like you, a people saved by the LORD? He is your protecting shield and your triumphant sword! Your enemies will cringe before you, and you will stomp on their backs!"* —Deuteronomy 33:29 (NLT)

Sometimes our greatest battles are those that are invisible to those around us. They are internal. My friend Natalia has such a story. As a little girl, she was sexually abused on a regular basis by an older male relative. For years, this man preyed on this precious girl in secret.

As an adult, Natalia saw a Christian counselor, and over time she healed from her childhood trauma. On one occasion, she knew she'd have to see her abuser at a family wedding. As the abusive man started to approach her, she held out her arm and shook her head, indicating for him not to move any closer. She stood up to him, and he turned away. Quietly and powerfully, Natalia was triumphant over her enemy. She stood courageously in Christ; as a result, her abuser lost his power.

Perhaps you, too, have endured abuse, harm, or cruelty from another person. If so, you can find protection and hope. Start with prayer and invite God to give you triumph over all that has hurt you. Then, talk with a trusted friend and maybe seek out the help of a mentor or counselor. You don't have to live in defeat, no matter what has been done to you.

Daily Declaration – *I declare that, in God, I am saved. He is my protective shield and my triumphant sword. My enemies will cringe before me, and I will stomp on their backs. No person, abuse, pain, or cruelty will steal my victory. I declare victory over my life—beginning today!*

Daily Prayer – *Lord, I know that you want me to live in hope, victory, and joy. Would you free me from anything that threatens to rob me of this victory? Would you perform a breakthrough in my life as I deal with past hurts and traumas? I need you today!*

Daily Action – According to one of my close friends, whose husband is a Christian counselor, about 33 percent of women have been abused and have talked about it. An additional 33 percent have been abused and have never shared it. Sixty-six percent. That's a lot of women! If you are in that group, today might be a good day to begin your journey of freedom. Consider writing a prayer and ask God to help you start the healing. (If you are blessed to be in the 34 percent of women who have not been abused, pray for a friend, roommate, or co-worker who may need to get help.)

The Lifter of Your Head

Daily Verse – *But You, O LORD, are a shield for me, my glory and the One who lifts up my head.* —Psalm 3:3 (NKJV)

When I was in high school, I played on my school's basketball team. Our team won a lot of games. Incidentally, we were one of the only girls' teams in the area that had two players over six feet tall. It was thrilling to be on an accomplished team that was known for winning so many games.

However, there were times when we played poorly and fell behind on the scoreboard. At halftime, we would head to the locker room for our pep talk and to have a chance to regroup. It was often during these moments when our coach would come into the locker room and find us with our heads down in discouragement. He then said something that changed everything. He would say, "Look up! Lift your heads! This game is not over yet!"

His words applied then and they apply now. In fact, they are scriptural. Our God is the lifter of our heads. He says to us today, "Look up! Lift your heads! This game is not over yet!"

Lift your head. No matter what is pulling you down, weighing on you, or crushing your heart today, refuse to believe that all is lost. This is not the day to give up. *Look up!* God wants to lift your head, your heart, and your heavy load today.

Daily Declaration – *I declare that God is my shield and the one who lifts my head. He can mend and repair the issues in my life. I will trust Him and lift my head again. Today, I will walk in victory, knowing I serve a God who is triumphant.*

Daily Prayer – *Lift my heart, head, and life today, Lord. I can so easily become bent over and discouraged. Would you lift me back up and get me back out there? I need you today.*

Daily Action – What is causing you to drop your head in discouragement today? What issues, relationships, and situations are keeping you from lifting your head? Write these out and pray over each one. God cares and wants to lift your head today.

God is Your Fence

Daily Verse – *As for God, his way is perfect: The LORD's word is flawless; he shields all who take refuge in him.* —Psalm 18:30 (NIV)

Years ago, researchers wanted to know whether the fences around playgrounds made children feel more secure. So they conducted a study of two playgrounds: one that was fenced in and the other that was not.

As they watched the children play on both playgrounds, they noticed stark differences. The children on the playground who lacked a fence remained on the playground equipment or around the surrounding areas. However, the children who were enclosed by a fence played freely across the entire play yard. These kids seemed less afraid and more carefree. The conclusion, as you can probably guess, was that the protective fence made the children feel more secure.[6]

In our lives, God is our protective shield. A shield can be a personal defensive weapon, but it can also be in the form of a fence, a surrounding wall of safety. Almighty God is like a huge hedge of protection in our lives. We can take refuge in Him and live more freely as He surrounds us with strength and grace.

As you go out into the world today, picture yourself fenced in and shielded by God. He surrounds you and protects you. You don't have to walk through this day alone!

Daily Declaration – *I declare that God's ways are perfect. His Word is flawless. He shields me as I take refuge in him. I will walk in victory today knowing that He surrounds and protects me. God is my shield, my wall of safety, and my hedge of protection.*

Daily Prayer – *Father, thank you for being my shield. Free me to walk without fear, without doubt, and in more confidence—knowing that you are with me. Thank you for surrounding me with hope, grace, and courage today.*

Daily Action – Are you encouraged to know that God is the fence of safety in your life? How will this make a difference for you today? Finish this thought in the space below: Because God is surrounding me with His love and protection, I...

....

....

....

....

....

....

....

....

....

....

....

....

....

Songs of Praise

Daily Verse – *David sang to the LORD the words of this song when the LORD delivered him from the hand of all his enemies and from the hand of Saul. He said: "The LORD is my rock, my fortress and my deliverer; my God is my rock, in whom I take refuge, my shield and the horn of my salvation. He is my stronghold, my refuge, and my savior—from violent people you save me. I called to the LORD, who is worthy of praise, and have been saved from my enemies."* —2 Samuel 22:1-4 (NIV)

Who doesn't love a service that is filled with incredible worship and praise music? Instruments that are in tune, beautiful voices singing powerful lyrics, and hands lifted high. If you are like me, perhaps you love to participate in a beautiful worship service as well.

Fortunately, we don't have to wait for Sundays before we worship. We can take a few moments today, wherever we are, and praise the God we love. By reading passages like the one above, we discover that David regularly broke out into song. He wrote music and lyrics, played music, and sang to the Lord.

Perhaps we need to do the same thing. Maybe we need to write a song of praise to God, play the song on an instrument, and sing a song of worship to Him. Even if you are not a singer, you can become a woman of great praise today. Praise God for who He is to you and thank Him for how He is blessing your life today.

Daily Declaration – *I declare that you are worthy of my praise, Lord. I will lift you up and honor your name. You are my rock, my fortress, my deliverer, my refuge, my shield, my salvation, and my Savior. I declare that you are worthy of great worship!*

Daily Prayer – *Lord, you are amazing, and I want to be a woman who recognizes your greatness. I praise you because you are absolutely worthy of my praise!*

Daily Action – Let's take a few moments to praise God for who He is. Go through the alphabet and assign a quality of God's that you admire for each letter. For example, *A* is for awesome, amazing, and able. *B* is for beautiful, blessed, and boundless. Jot down these traits. Then, go through each one and praise God for these qualities of His.

Waiting Quietly for God

Daily Verse – *I stand silently to listen for the one I love, waiting as long as it takes for the Lord to rescue me. For God alone has become my Savior. He alone is my safe place; his wraparound presence always protects me. For he is my champion defender; there's no risk of failure with God. So why would I let worry paralyze me, even when troubles multiply around me?* —Psalm 62:1-2 (TPT)

When I played basketball in high school, our coach would make the team spread across the locker room and sit quietly before a game. It felt like hours passed, but it usually it was only ten minutes. During this quiet time, we were told to take deep breaths, visualize the game plan, visualize our shots going in, and pray about the upcoming match. Although my mind often drifted during this quiet time, it did serve to calm my nerves before each game.

Similarly, in the Christian life, there may come times when we need to sit silently before the Lord. We need to take the time to wait upon the Lord, rest in His presence, and allow Him to calm our nerves. When troubles multiply and worry paralyzes us, let's spend time with the Lord.

What does this look like? For me, it sometimes requires that I wear my earbuds, even though I don't turn on any music. Sometimes, however, I may just turn on soft music. At times, I remain still and picture God wrapping His arms around me. Maybe you need to lift your head to heaven or raise your hands in surrender. Primarily, the goal of this time is for us to focus our attention on God and allow His presence to wrap around us.

Daily Declaration – *I declare that God is my Savior and my safe place. As I sit quietly before Him, I enjoy His wraparound presence and protection. He is my champion defender and the One who calms my worries and grants me true success.*

Daily Prayer – *Would you help me spend more quiet moments with you, Lord? I want to remember to look to you, focus on you, and remain aware of you more often. Direct my heart and attention to you. I need you!*

Daily Action – Do you spend time each day sitting quietly before the Lord? What does that look like with your schedule? Brainstorm four or five creative ways you can spend more quiet time with God. For example, maybe you can take a quiet walk, listen to quiet praise music, or take five minutes to stop and pray. Jot these ideas in the space below. Then, try one of these ideas today.

God Wants to Know You

Daily Verse – *This is the account of the heavens and the earth when they were created, when the LORD God made the earth and the heavens.* —Genesis 2:4 (NIV)

Every couple of weeks, I meet with a woman named Barbara who is one of my favorite older friends and mentors. Every time she sees me, she never fails to tell me how beautiful I look. Then, she asks questions and listens to my responses. I know Barbara enjoys spending time with me, and this makes me want to spend even more time with her.

Do you have a friend, mentor, or family member who makes you feel beautiful? Special? Loved? Enjoyed? Is there someone you are drawn to because of how they seem to enjoy spending time with you? If so, you are greatly blessed. If not, consider asking God to send you encouraging friends and mentors.

Jehovah God is a relational God. He is great and mighty, but He also wants to spend time with you. He wants to hear your heart, talk to you, and tell you how beautiful you are to Him. The God of the Bible desires to know you and to become known by you. One of His greatest desires is to have a close relationship with you.

Daily Declaration – *I declare that the Lord of this universe wants to have a close relationship with me. He loves me and wants to spend time with me. My God will reveal himself to me as I spend time with Him.*

Daily Prayer – *Lord, sometimes I get so busy that I don't spend time with you. Thank you that you never leave me nor forsake me. You are always available to spend time with me. Draw me closer to you. Help me to know you more and to enjoy our relationship more.*

Daily Action – Who makes you feel valued and special? Is there a friend, co-worker, mentor, or family member who encourages and builds you up? Have you ever thought about how God wants to have a close relationship with you? How does this make you feel? Reflect on how you can make your relationship with God more of a priority today.

....

....

....

....

....

....

....

....

....

....

....

....

....

What is Your Calling?

Daily Verse – *There the angel of the LORD appeared to him in flames of fire from within a bush. Moses saw that though the bush was on fire it did not burn up ... "Do not come any closer," God said. "Take off your sandals, for the place where you are standing is holy ground." Then he said, "I am the God of your father, the God of Abraham, the God of Isaac and the God of Jacob." At this, Moses hid his face, because he was afraid to look at God.* —Exodus 3:2,5-6 (NIV)

In one of the most interesting passages of the Bible, God called Moses by using a burning bush. God lit the bush on fire, but it did not burn up. On a regular weekday, and in the middle of nowhere—while Moses took care of sheep—God showed up. From then on, nothing was the same for Moses.

My life-changing moment happened at church camp when I was in the ninth grade. During a weekday service, God called me to serve Him with my life. I began to write materials for Lifeway Christian resources. Then, I wrote articles for magazines and books. Finally, God provided a way for me to publish blog posts and books. Some four hundred blog posts and nine books later, I'm still amazed at how God works!

How about you? Did you know that God has a "calling" upon your life? Each of us is called to serve the Lord and to make a difference for Him on this planet. God wants to use you and your unique gifts and talents! So, how has God approached you and gotten your attention? How has He spoken to your heart? How might God want to use you? This is a great thing to prayerfully consider.

Daily Declaration – *I declare that God has called me to do amazing things for Him and His kingdom. He has great plans to use me. I will surrender to His plans and put my "yes" on the table for His glory and honor. I want to get in on whatever God is doing.*

Daily Prayer – *Father, I thank you that you have awesome plans to use my life for your purposes. Thank you that you have allowed me to live at this time in history. Thank you that I can make a difference in the lives of others.*

Daily Action – What does your calling look like? What are three or four ways you are specially created and gifted to make a difference for the kingdom of God? Maybe you are interested in music, writing, art, speaking, missions, sports, working with kids, politics, medicine, teaching, etc. Brainstorm some of these ideas in the space below.

God Will Meet You

Daily Verse – *My God in His faithfulness will meet me; God will let me look triumphantly upon my enemies.* —Psalm 59:10 (NASB)

At the funeral of Billy Graham, his daughter Ruth shared about her evangelist father and the impact that he had on her life. On one occasion, she realized she had really blown it. She had a messy divorce and then hopped into another bad relationship. The whole family warned her against this new man. But she started to date him anyway.

To make a long story short, things turned sour. Ruth headed back to her parents' home, embarrassed and heartbroken. As she drove along the long driveway to their home, she saw her daddy standing in the driveway. He wrapped his arms around her and welcomed her home … No shame. No lectures. Ruth received nothing less than grace and unconditional love from her father.[7]

All of us have had times in our lives when we blew it. We all make mistakes. We choose poorly. And yet the Bible tells us that God's faithfulness will meet us. As we drive up God's driveway and get out of the car, our loving God will wrap His arms around us and welcome us home. No shame or lectures. No condemnation. Only grace and unconditional love.

Daily Declaration – *I declare that my God will always faithfully meet me with love. No matter what I have done or how much I have messed up, my heavenly Father will welcome me home. I will arise and go to Jesus. He will embrace me in His arms.[8]*

Daily Prayer – *Oh, God. I am so glad that I don't have to run or hide from you when I blow it. I can always turn to you. In fact, when I sin, fail, and mess up, would you help me turn to you sooner?*

Daily Action – Often, in our humanness, we run away from God when we sin or make a mistake. But God calls us to come home and return to His embrace—especially during times when we blow it. Why don't you talk to God about this? What has been keeping you from coming to Him? Is there anything driving a wedge between you and God lately? Write a prayer below and share your heart.

Ever Been Wronged by Someone Else?

Daily Verse – *Live, GOD! Blessings from my Rock, my free and freeing God, towering! This God set things right for me and shut up the people who talked back. He rescued me from enemy anger, he pulled me from the grip of upstarts. He saved me from the bullies.* —Psalm 18:46-48 (MSG)

Have you ever been wrongly accused? Mistreated? Slandered? Made fun of? Betrayed? Misled? Misunderstood? Hurt by someone else? If you walk on this planet long enough, you will likely experience all of these injustices and more. You can't live among people without facing occasional conflict, pain, and bad treatment.

But there is hope amid injustice. We serve a God who sees all things. And He will set things right and silence those who have spoken against us. The Bible tells us that the Lord will rescue us, free us from our enemies, and save us from bullies.

So what do we do when we find ourselves on the receiving end of someone's spiteful behavior?

It may be challenging, but we can find victory by:

1. Showing restraint. We don't need to try and get even.
2. Forgiving the other person. Let's ask God to drain our anger.
3. Venting about them to God (rather than gossiping to others).
4. Allowing God to balance the scales and deal with your offender the way He sees fit.

Daily Declaration – *I declare that my God is just and able to fight my battles for me. He will avenge me. I don't need to seek my own revenge; instead, I can trust God to be El Nekamoth, the God who avenges me.*

Daily Prayer – *God, you are a great and fair avenger. You can and will deal with those who hurt me. Help me to restrain myself, forgive my offender, and release them to you. Your justice is more effective than anything I might do in response to this offense.*

Daily Action – Have you ever thought about how God is your Avenger? How does this encourage you? Is there someone or something you need him to avenge for you today? Tell God about this situation. He already knows, but it will do you good to share your pain. Ask God to perform whatever He wants to carry out in this situation according to His will.

But They Did Me Wrong!

Daily Verse – *Never repay evil for evil to anyone. Respect what is right in the sight of all people. If possible, so far as it depends on you, be at peace with all people. Never take your own revenge, beloved, but leave room for the wrath of God, for it is written: "VENGEANCE IS MINE, I WILL REPAY," says the Lord.*
—Romans 12:17-19 (NASB)

Naomi (not her real name) was one of the most beautiful and popular girls in the large high school I attended. She had flowing dark hair and eyes, as well as a perfect figure. Naomi had the complete package—cheerleader, intelligent, and the like. And yet she was one of the meanest girls I ever met. She was always stealing someone's boyfriend and manipulating situations to her advantage. No one could trust her.

She was also my longtime friend, so it was impossible for me to avoid Naomi and her venom—but I quickly learned how to deal with her:

I prayed for her. I chose carefully what I shared with her, and I trusted God to be the judge. Even though there were times when I wanted to retaliate, I chose to avoid repaying evil for her evil. I dealt with Naomi in grace, allowing God to handle her and her issues.

Years later, I honestly feel sorry for Naomi. She hasn't lived a happy life since we graduated high school. She's dealt with failed marriages. Difficulty at work. Broken relationships. Hurt and pain. She has lived a difficult life. (And I still pray for her.)

Daily Declaration – *I declare that I don't need to repay evil to anyone. I can do right, live in peace, and leave room for the wrath of God. He will repay and get justice. It's not in my hands.*

Daily Prayer – *Lord, would you enable me to leave room for your wrath? Give me the grace to avoid repaying evil for evil and help me to respect others and treat them with grace. When I am mistreated by others, I will give them over to you. You are wise and perfectly capable of doling out the proper justice.*

Daily Action – What did you think of my story about Naomi? Have you been on the receiving end of bullying, deceit, or manipulation by someone else? If you hand this person over to God, how do you think He will deal with them?

....

....

....

....

....

....

....

....

....

....

....

....

Perfectly Woven Together

Daily Verse – *But each day the LORD pours his unfailing love upon me, and through each night I sing his songs, praying to God who gives me life.* —Psalm 42:8 (NLT)

My grandmother was an amazing seamstress. With a needle and thread, she could whip together a masterpiece. She did counted cross stitch and crocheted. Every piece that my grandmother created was beautiful—intricate in detail and quite fantastic. As a child, I tried to follow in her footsteps, but I never quite mastered her skillful stitchery.

Our God is the God of the very fabric of our lives. With His skillful hand, He weaves together the events, people, places, and details of our lives while He pours out His unfailing love.

He is an expert at threading together the hours, days, weeks, and months that make up our life. Nothing escapes His notice. Nothing gets out of His earshot. Not one detail is missed.

Your God has perfect plans for your life, and He knows which steps you should take next. He will illuminate the darkness of your path and direct you in the days ahead. As you finish school, take that first job, choose your major, decide about relationships, and study for exams, God is beside you—day and night. You can trust Him and depend on Him.

Daily Declaration – *I declare that you are my God, totally interested in the details, issues, and minutia of my life. No one loves me as much as you do. You are the God who infuses me with life and pours unfailing love on me. I trust my future to you.*

Daily Prayer – *Thank you, Lord, for being the God of my life. You are God of my past, my present, and my future. Help me to look to you and to trust you more than I ever have before.*

Daily Action – Let's talk about your future. What's next on your agenda for today? What are you looking forward to this summer? Next year? Do you have any plans for what your life will look like in five years? Take a moment and write three or four future endeavors that you are looking forward to. Then, talk to God about each one. Invite Him to give you wisdom and to shed His light on each of your plans.

God is My Help

Daily Verse – *Save me, O God, by your name; vindicate me by your might. Hear my prayer, O God; listen to the words of my mouth … Surely God is my help; the Lord is the one who sustains me.* —Psalm 54:1-2, 4 (NIV)

Quick! Name the most dependable person you know. Maybe it's a sister, a friend, your mom or dad, a teacher, or a grandparent. Got the person in mind? Good. Now, why did you think of this person? What makes this person dependable in your life? What do you most appreciate about their dependability?

Have you ever considered the dependability of God? The Bible tells us that God is our dependable help (Elohim Ozer Li). He doesn't take a vacation, leave the office, take a nap, check out, cut the connection, lose bandwidth, or fall asleep. He is always on call and available to us. Almighty God is our helper and the most dependable person in the world.

When you face homesickness, God is available. When you feel pressure, doubt, or insecurity, God is your help. If you feel lonely or left out, look to God. Lacking inspiration? Not sure what to do next? Turn to God. As you turn to Him, He offers to sustain you, bolster you, buoy you, defend you, assist you, and help you. What do you need from your dependable God today?

Daily Declaration – *I declare that God is my helper. He is utterly and completely dependable and available to me. I can turn to Him at all times. The Lord is indeed the one who hears me, sustains me, vindicates me, and protects me.*

Daily Prayer – *Thank you, Lord, for being my helper, the one I can turn to at all times. I'm grateful for your help, your support, and your encouragement. Rather than waiting until I'm desperate, remind me to turn to you sooner and more often.*

Daily Action – How do you need God to be your helper today? What do you need from Him today? Make a list of your relationships, projects, prayer requests, and issues that could use the touch of God today. Then, invite Him to help you with each of these areas.

Great and Mighty, Yet Personal

Daily Verse – *"Sovereign LORD, you have begun to show to your servant your greatness and your strong hand. For what god is there in heaven or on earth who can do the deeds and mighty works you do?"* —Deuteronomy 3:24 (NIV)

Not long ago, the most unusual thing happened to me. My husband and I were at church, helping to set up for an event, when someone tapped me on the shoulder. I turned around, assuming it was a church friend. Instead, I stood face-to-face with one of my heroes in the faith. Josh McDowell, an international speaker and author of over one hundred and fifty books, talked with me and asked me about my life. I was absolutely blown away!

Perhaps you've had the chance to meet someone you admire or someone famous—maybe at your high school, college, church, or while traveling. It's an awesome experience, isn't it?

Have you thought about how the Creator and Lord of the universe wants to have a personal relationship with you? He is great and mighty, strong, and capable, and yet He knows how many hairs are on your head. He knows what you ate for breakfast and what kind of coffee you prefer. This mighty God is personally interested in your concerns, cares, worries, and fears. While continuing to control the world and command the stars, Gods bends down to listen to your prayers.

Daily Declaration – *I declare that the great and mighty God also cares about me. He is deeply concerned about my wellbeing. Yes, he is Adonai—the master over all things. And yet, He is near to me. He is with me. And He is for me. It's unexplainable and awesome, all at the same time.*

Daily Prayer – *Thank you, God, for creating and mastering the mountains, oceans, forests, planets, and me. Your power is mesmerizing, and your heart is kind at the same time. You are over all things, and yet you still have time for me. That is sweet!*

Daily Action – Who is the most famous person you have ever met? What made the meeting special? How does it encourage you to know that Almighty God is uniquely interested in your life? Write about how this truth makes you feel.

Will We Surrender?

Daily Verse – *Let them praise the name of the LORD, for his name alone is exalted; his splendor is above the earth and the heavens.* —Psalm 148:13 (NIV)

My husband and I attended a convention in Nashville, Tennessee, and stayed in a beautiful hotel that had amazing service. As the bellhop helped to place our bags in the car, my husband checked out. He opened the passenger door for me and asked an unusual question, "Why do you suppose men usually drive instead of women?"

I gave him a funny smile and said, "I think it's because we let them."

As couples grow older, however, we often see little old women driving around little old men. But during the earlier years of dating, relationships, and marriage, men are almost always the drivers. Obviously, women are well able to drive—but we often defer to our men, surrender control of the steering wheel and allow our guys to chauffeur us around.

What about with God? How hard is it for us to give up control? Do we see God as the One who alone is exalted and above all things? Will we spiritually give Him charge of the steering wheel of our life and allow Jesus to take the wheel?

Daily Declaration – *I declare that God alone is exalted. His splendor is above the heavens and the earth. Because he is Master and Lord over all, I can trust him to take complete control over my life.*

Daily Prayer – *Father, I want to trust you to be Lord of my life, steering and driving me anywhere you want me to go. I know I could steer my own life if I wanted, but I much prefer to go in your direction instead of my own. I surrender. I give you the keys!*

Daily Action – Do you have any control issues? Do you like to be in charge? Giving over control can be a challenge for us all. In the space below, list one or two areas of your life where you know you have given God control. Thank him for blessing your surrender. Then, list one or two areas of your life that you seem to be holding onto. Invite God to enable you to give these to Him as well.

Perfectly Tuned

Daily Verse – *He went a little farther and fell on His face, and prayed, saying, "O My Father, if it is possible, let this cup pass from Me; nevertheless, not as I will, but as You will." —Matthew 26:39 (NKJV)*

Have you ever heard an orchestra or a symphony play live music? Before the production begins, the pianist strikes an *A* note, and the other instrumentalists tune their instruments to that note. Every instrument seeks to get in tune with the other instruments so that their collective music sounds marvelous.

In our Christian walk, we must also regularly tune our lives to the *A* string of heaven. As heaven strikes the perfect note, we should tune our lives with this note. It's a form of surrender.

Just as Jesus surrendered His life to death on a cross, we must also surrender our lives to whatever God calls us to do. Most days, it's as simple as the prayer Jesus prayed: "If possible, let this cup pass from me. Nevertheless, not my will but yours be done."

To say this prayer is to completely trust God with our lives. Pastor Adrian Rogers once said, "God only wants for us what we would want for ourselves if we were smart enough to want it."[9]

Daily Declaration – *I declare that God is trustworthy. I can tune my life with His will and trust that He will do what is best for me. I declare that God always wants the best for my life and for my future.*

Daily Prayer – *Father, I want to surrender and trust in your will. I know that you want what is best for me—in my career, schooling, relationships, finances, future, and in all areas of my life. Help me to remember this.*

Daily Action – Make a list of the seven to ten most important areas of your life right now. This may include work, school, a romantic relationship, friendships, church, health, finances, etc. Then, pray over each area like this: "Lord, I'd love to see [fill in the blank here] happen, but I refuse to press for my will. Instead, I ask that you have your way in this area. I surrender this to you."

Impossible Situations

Daily Verse – *When Abram was ninety-nine years old, the LORD appeared to him and said, "I am El-Shaddai—'God Almighty.' Serve me faithfully and live a blameless life. I will make a covenant with you, by which I will guarantee to give you countless descendants."* —Genesis 17:1-2 (NLT)

Have you found yourself in an impossible situation lately? Maybe it was with a friend, parent, or job. Or maybe you've recently faced difficulties with a class, with money, or any other private battle you might be fighting. Life is full of impossible situations. We all face moments when we wonder, "How will I get through this? How will this possibly work out for good?"

In our verses today, Abram found himself in an impossible situation. At ninety-nine years old, he still wanted to have children and grandchildren. Pretty unlikely. Until God showed up. Almighty God 'El Shaddai' stepped onto the scene, and everything changed. God told Abram to live a faithful life in service to the Lord, and he would be blessed with countless children and grandchildren.

In your situation today, God also wants to perform the impossible. He is El Shaddai, the All-Sufficient God. Stocked with unlimited supplies and resources, nothing is too hard for Him. If Abram and Sarai could be blessed with children at their old age, then you, too, can have your needs met. Your God can take care of you—no matter what is going on. Trust that He is able!

Daily Declaration – *I declare that God is Almighty. He is El Shaddai, the All-Sufficient One. No matter what seems impossible, irredeemable, uncurable, irreconcilable, or unfixable, nothing gets past my God. He takes care of me.*

Daily Prayer – *Honestly, Lord, sometimes I'm tempted to look at the impossible situations and become overwhelmed at their size before I look to you and remember that you are greater. Help me to come to you first and be encouraged, El Shaddai. Then, we can look at the challenges together.*

Daily Action – Let's talk about impossible situations. What seems most unlikely and most impossible to you right now? Why do you feel this way? Take a few moments and write a prayer to God. Pour your heart out and invite Him to fix, repair, amend, restore, or heal your situation.

Miracles Still Take Place!

Daily Verse – *Then the twenty-four elders who sit on their thrones before God fell facedown before him and worshiped him, saying: "We give thanks to you, Lord God Almighty, who is, and who was, because you have established your great and limitless power and begun to reign!"* —Revelation 11:16-17 (TPT)

My husband and I needed $2000 to pay for a car repair bill, but the money just wasn't available. So, we prayed for a miracle. It was the first thing I did every morning after I awoke. I'd pray. Before my husband and I went to bed, we'd pray. As the deadline to pay this amount grew closer, we prayed even more.

Then, the craziest week of miracles occurred. One week, on a Tuesday, we received a check for $400 as a repayment for money we had loaned. On Wednesday, more money came in from a company my husband had previously worked for.

The total? $300. Then, on Friday, we received a refund from a hospital bill that we had overpaid. (This never happens!) The amount? $1300. In one week, and just in time, God sent us $2000 in the mail. The exact amount we needed. As you can imagine, we were blown away by His goodness.

Have you ever asked God for a miracle? He is the Lord God Almighty—the One who has great and limitless power. Why not invite Him to display His power in your life? I challenge you to ask Him to bless you in unexpected ways. He is so good.

Daily Declaration – *I declare that I am going to trust God more. God is great and powerful and able to perform miracles. As His daughter, I want to see more of His miraculous power in my life. I invite Him to bless me and surprise me with His goodness.*

Daily Prayer – *Lord, forgive me for placing limits on you. I want that to change today. I want to pray bigger, expect bigger, and hope bigger, and I invite you to do more in, with, and through my life. You are El Shaddai. Thank you that you are great and mighty! Thank you for your goodness and for all you are about to do.*

Daily Action – Are you ready to step out in faith? I want to encourage you to pray bigger, believe bigger, and trust God like you never have before. In the space below, write two or three brave prayer requests. What would you love to see God do in your life? How do you want Him to work? What miracles would you love to see occur in your life?

My Exceeding Joy

Daily Verse – *Then I will come closer to your very altar until I come before you, the God of my ecstatic joy! I will praise you with the harp that plays in my heart to you, my God, my magnificent God!*
—Psalm 43:4 (TPT)

When you think of the word *joy*, what comes to mind? Great happiness? Sheer pleasure? An incredible sense of delight, exhilaration, and fun? We often lump the concepts of joy and happiness into the same group. But biblical joy is far deeper than momentary happiness.

Joy is a byproduct of God's overflowing goodness, which bubbles up from inside of us. It's a deep reservoir of trust that causes us to have hope, peace, and purpose in life. We can have great joy even when life is hard.

How can we obtain this joy? By drawing close to the altar of God and spending time with Him.

Our God is the God of ecstatic joy. He offers exceeding joy and gladness to all who spend time in His presence.

Receiving God's joy is like drinking a refreshing glass of water on a hot day or sipping on a steaming cup of coffee on a freezing cold morning. God's joy is like that cozy feeling you may experience on a Saturday morning after hitting "snooze" on your alarm and snuggling back beneath the covers to sleep in. It's sweet. It's comforting. It's refreshing. It's restorative. It's real. Have you experienced this joy?

Daily Declaration – *I declare that my God is the God of incredible joy. When I hang out with Him regularly, I will be full of His joy. My life will overflow with joy because of Him.*

Daily Prayer – *Thank you, Lord, for giving us great joy as we come close to you. You are the God of ecstatic joy! You are El Simchath Gili. I praise you and bless you for being such a magnificent God!*

Daily Action – Think about the concept of joy. How is joy different than happiness? How have you personally experienced God's ecstatic joy? Write about this in the space below.

The Lord is My Shepherd

Daily Verse – *The LORD is my shepherd, I lack nothing. He makes me lie down in green pastures, he leads me beside quiet waters, he refreshes my soul. He guides me along the right path for his name's sake. Even though I walk through the darkest valley, I will fear no evil, for you are with me; your rod and your staff, they comfort me. You prepare a table before me in the presence of my enemies. You anoint my head with oil, my cup overflows. Surely your goodness and love will follow me all the days of my life, and I will dwell in the house of the LORD forever.* —Psalm 23 (NIV)

Today's passage is a favorite for many people. We love to think about God as our Shepherd who keeps watch over us, guides us, protects us, provides for us, and keeps track of us. The image of a strong, compassionate, and good shepherd reminds us that our Heavenly Father watches out for us and takes good care of us. It's encouraging, isn't it?

Perhaps you are unsure of what should come next in your life, in your college career, in your job, with your dating life, or in your future in general. It's possible that you have been praying for God to lead and guide you forward, but things are still unclear and unsettled.

Can I offer a prayer suggestion? It comes from one of my mentors named Christie. She regularly prays this prayer: "Lord, would you be my Shepherd who stands clearly where I can see you? I'm just a dumb sheep, and I don't want to miss you." Why not begin to pray this way as well?

Daily Declaration – *I declare that God is my Shepherd, and I lack nothing. He leads me and refreshes my soul. He guides me, protects me, and fills my cup. His goodness will follow me all the days of life until I enter heaven. I trust in my Good Shepherd.*

Daily Prayer – *Thank you for being my Shepherd, Jehovah Rohi. I'm grateful that I can follow where you lead. You are so trustworthy and capable. Would you give me the grace to trust you more?*

Daily Action – How do you need God to lead and guide you today? Where do you have uncertainty or confusion? What decisions are you trying to make? Consider praying the prayer included in today's devotion.

....

....

....

....

....

....

....

....

....

....

....

....

....

....

God Gently Carries Us in His Arms

Daily Verse – *He will care for you as a shepherd tends his flock, gathering the weak lambs and taking them in his arms. He carries them close to his heart and gently leads those that have young.* —Isaiah 40:11 (TPT)

Have you ever seen, on the news or the Internet, a story about a fireman who rescued a child or small animal from a burning building? The fireman cradles that child or animal close to his heart as he moves them to safety.

As our Shepherd, our great God tends to the flock. He gathers the weakest lambs into His arms and carries them close to His heart. Snuggled close in His grasp, His flock is loved, cared for, and comforted.

If you are feeling weak, snuggle in close to your Shepherd. Even though you can't see or touch Him, you can be held close and comforted. Use your sanctified imagination and picture God gathering you in His powerful arms and holding you close to His heart. He adores you and wants to offer you comfort, hope, and compassion today. Press in and allow Him to hold you.

Daily Declaration – *I declare that my Shepherd is looking out for me—especially when I feel weak, exhausted, and needy. He will pick me up, hold me close, and carry me. He notices my weaknesses and has great compassion on me.*

Daily Prayer – *Thank you for being the kind of shepherd that is aware and interested in your flock. You are Jehovah Rohi. I'm so grateful that you hold us close on our hard days. You are an amazing caretaker, and I love you.*

Daily Action – As you think about snuggling up close to God today, what would you like to say to Him? Write a prayer to Him, sharing your greatest struggles, hurts, and challenges. Invite God to comfort and strengthen your weaknesses.

God Lights Your Path

Daily Verse – *O LORD, you are my lamp. The LORD lights up my darkness.* —2 Samuel 22:29 (NLT)

Figuring out what we should do next is sometimes a great challenge.

We are faced with many decisions in life. Some are small, like what we should eat for lunch, what outfit we should wear, how long we should study, and whether we will work out today. Others are larger. For example, you may be deciding on what major to declare, who to marry, where to live, or whether or not to take a particular job. Life is filled with choices.

That's why it's encouraging to know that God is our light. He is our lamp who lights the darkness. We don't have to figure everything out on our own. Instead, we serve a God who offers great direction. He is wiser than any GPS bot— such as Siri, Google Map, or Waze. You serve a God who reveals, illuminates, and enlightens. He loves to shed light onto your path.

One word of wisdom on this matter comes from one of my mentors, Dr. Anita Baker. When speaking of God's leading, she once told me, "God doesn't usually lead with a neon sign, huge spotlight, or even a large flashlight. Typically, God leads with a small penlight, one small step at a time. So, you must walk close to Him so you can know where to step next."

Daily Declaration – *I declare that my God is a lamp. He lights up my darkness. As I walk close to Him, I will have clear direction and know which steps to take next.*

Daily Prayer – *Thank you, Lord, for being my lamp and my light. You are my lamp. Knowing that you reveal, enlighten, illuminate, and light up the darkness gives me hope. Would you keep me close to your side so I can clearly see where to walk next?*

Daily Action – Think about the decisions you make every day. What are three or four small choices you have already made so far today? What are a few big decisions you may have in front of you now? Write them in the space below. Then, go back over each one and invite God to shine His light and provide guidance on how you can best handle each one.

God is the Revealer of Mysteries

Daily Verse – *Daniel replied, "No wise man, enchanter, magician or diviner can explain to the king the mystery he has asked about, but there is a God in heaven who reveals mysteries. He has shown King Nebuchadnezzar what will happen in days to come. Your dream and the visions that passed through your mind as you were lying in bed are these."* —Daniel 2:27-28 (NIV)

The situation was complicated. Two of my close friends were upset with each other and I was caught in the middle. I understood both sides, and I believed that both of them needed to make concessions. However, as the conflict continued for a couple of weeks, I grew weary. And then I read today's verses. Specifically, I was drawn to the phrase that says, "there is a God in heaven who reveals mysteries."

I began to pray to God, the revealer of mysteries, asking Him for wisdom and discernment about how to move forward with my friends who were engaged in this conflict. I prayed daily, and God showed me ideas, verses, and guidance about what I could do and say in the situation. As I prayed and searched, God sent solutions that solved the mystery.

Do you also have challenging situations, relationships, and mysteries in your life? Why not invite God to reveal ideas, solutions, and wise responses to you? He is willing and able.

Daily Declaration – *I declare that my God is the revealer of mysteries. He is able to show me secrets, solutions, and wise responses to all things. As I spend time in the Bible, in worship, with wise friends, and in prayer, God will make known to me all of the explanations that I need.*

Daily Prayer – *Thank you, God, for being Gelah Raz, the revealer of mysteries. Just as Daniel trusted you to interpret dreams, I will trust you to show me incredible truths, ideas, and solutions.*

Daily Action – Consider your own life right now. Where do you need God to reveal mysteries and secrets? Where do you need wisdom? Pray about the issue that needs the most attention today. Invite God to give you verses, conversations, song lyrics, sermons, podcasts, and thoughts that will make you wiser in this situation.

God Will Show You Great and Mighty Things

Daily Verse – *This is what the LORD says, he who made the earth, the LORD who formed it and established it—the LORD is his name: "Call to me and I will answer you and tell you great and unsearchable things you do not know."* —Jeremiah 33:2-3 (NIV)

Mrs. Hardy has been teaching the Bible at my church for decades. Soft-spoken, humble, and kind, you would not immediately take this woman for being a great Bible scholar. However, her command of the Scriptures, truth, and biblical principles is impressive. I enjoyed spending one-on-one time with her.

In one of our mentoring sessions, Mrs. Hardy suggested something interesting to me about God's will. Rather than going on a hunt for God's will, her teaching was much simpler. She said I would discover God's great plans for me as I was going—praying, reading the Bible, listening to inspirational music, worshipping, reading, and living.

God will do the same for you. Call on Him and invite Him to show you great and mighty things that you don't yet know. Ask Him to reveal what you should do next, how to handle a situation, and what He has in store for you. Then, do the next things. Read the Bible. Pray. Worship. Listen to great podcasts. God can speak in your daily life as you are *going*.

Daily Declaration – *I declare that God will speak to me. He will show me what I do not know about things to come. He will grant me wisdom and show me all that I need to know as I live my life and look to him.*

Daily Prayer – *Father, I want to know great and mighty things about what is to come. Be the revealer of secrets, the One who shows me how to proceed. You are Gelah Riz, and you will show me all I need to know.*

Daily Action – In what ways has God shown you great and mighty things in the past? Share an example in the space below. Where do you need wisdom and insight today? As you invite God to speak to you, be on the lookout for His instructions. As you read His Word, worship, and pray, expect God to speak to you!

The God Who Heals

Daily Verse – *He said, "If you listen carefully to the LORD your God and do what is right in his eyes, if you pay attention to his commands and keep all his decrees, I will not bring on you any of the diseases I brought on the Egyptians, for I am the LORD, who heals you." —Exodus 15:26 (NIV)*

The symptoms were always the same: extreme fatigue, bad headache, sore throat, and joint pain. For years, Emily dealt with this unexplainable illness without knowing the cause. Doctor after doctor misdiagnosed her symptoms as vitamin deficiency, chronic fatigue, or some sort of autoimmune disease.

One day, as her mom prayed with a group of ladies, a breakthrough occurred. One of the ladies had been to a doctor who practiced innovative medicine and advised diet changes and various supplements to treat patients. His protocols helped many people become well. After much prayer, Emily and her mom went to see this doctor. Within a few weeks, Emily's health returned, and healing took place. God provided healing through an unorthodox physician.

God is a God who heals. He restores health, emotions, relationships, churches, marriages, bank accounts, and much more. With just one word, God can remove sickness, reverse disease, breathe life, and bring forth healing. How do you need His healing touch today?

Daily Declaration – *I declare that you are Jehovah Rophe, the God who heals. You are able to heal, and I trust you to heal me and make me whole. As I follow you wholeheartedly, I trust you to be the great Physician in my life.*

Daily Prayer – *I praise you for being the God who heals. You are well able to mend, restore, renew, renovate, reestablish, revive, and remaster anyone and anything. Help me to turn to you sooner for healing.*

Daily Action – Where do you need healing today? Invite God to work in your broken places. Then, pray for a few friends or family members who need healing as well. Be specific as you lift them up in prayer. You can use the space below to write these requests.

God is Our Hope

Daily Verse – *But those who hope in the LORD will renew their strength. They will soar on wings like eagles; they will run and not grow weary; they will walk and not be faint.* —Isaiah 40:31 (NIV)

Seven years ago, my husband and I launched our ministry and named it "Hope Ministry." Our mission is to share genuine hope to others. We don't suggest that people use wishful thinking, wish on a star, or believe in a pipe dream. Instead, our passion is to point people back to the strong, rock-ribbed, and powerful assurance of hope we find in relationship with God Almighty.

We do not have a shaky faith. Rather, this faith is strong and sure because it is based on a strong and sure God. He is Miqweh Yisreal, the Hope of Israel and the hope of every believer in Jesus Christ. The Bible promises that those who hope in the Lord will find renewed strength. They will soar like eagles, not growing weary or fainting.

What are you placing your hope in today? Your friends? Your job or career? Your family? Your education? Your boyfriend or fiancé? Your church or pastor? Your finances or bank account? Politicians or world leaders? Yourself? Honestly, none of these people or things are worthy of our hope. Instead, let's direct our hope to God and God alone! Everyone and everything else is temporary, fleeting, and not worthy of our total trust. God, however, is completely safe, durable, and dependable.

Daily Declaration – *I declare that God is worthy of my complete hope and dependance. I can hope in Him. I can trust in Him. Just as He is the Hope of Israel, He is my hope as well.*

Daily Prayer – *Father, would you help me trust you, look to you, and lean on you? I really do want to place my hope in you. Would you boost my faith and help my unbelief? Give me the grace I need to trust you more.*

Daily Action – Honesty time: Where do you typically direct your greatest hope? Do you place your hope in humans rather than God? If so, what keeps you from trusting Him more? Share about this in the space below. Discuss your doubts with the Lord. Share your heart with Him.

The Lord is My Lifelong Confidence

Daily Verse – *But blessed is the one who trusts in the LORD, whose confidence is in him. They will be like a tree planted by the water that sends out its roots by the stream. It does not fear when heat comes; its leaves are always green. It has no worries in a year of drought and never fails to bear fruit.* —Jeremiah 17:7-8 (NIV)

Dr. Gray Allison was my evangelism professor at seminary, and he was a ninety-year-old man who still followed God wholeheartedly. Quick-witted, passionate, and wise, this man lived his entire life completely confident in the God he served. In fact, I believe Dr. Gray became more excited about his calling with each passing year.

At his funeral, one person after another talked about the incredible faith this man of God had. No, Dr. Gray Allison wasn't perfect, but he was grounded and full of hope and life. Even at an old age he impacted lives, shared the Gospel, and made a difference for the kingdom of God.

The close relationship he built with God at a young age affected the entire trajectory of his life.

What might happen if you made God your hope and your confidence now? What if you began to really trust God and were determined to follow Him all the days of your life? I don't know about you, but I someday want to be a little old lady who still serves the Lord, loves other people, and makes a difference for the kingdom of God.

Daily Declaration – *I declare that God is my hope and my confidence. As I place my faith in Him, He will make me like a tree planted by the water whose roots go deep. I will not fear the heat or the droughts that might come. I will trust God to keep me strong and to keep me growing.*

Daily Prayer – *Lord, I want to live in complete confidence and hope in you. You are trustworthy. And I want to follow you all my life until I am a little old lady. Will you enable me to do this?*

Daily Action – Think about some of the senior adults you love and respect—maybe your grandparents, a Bible teacher, or a preacher. Write their names in the space below and share a couple of reasons why you respect them. Then, ask God to build into your life the same character traits that you admire in these seniors.

What About Truth?

Daily Verse – *I give my spirit into Your hands. You have made me free, O Lord, God of truth.* —Psalm 31:5 (NLV)

Truth is hard to find these days. Whether on the news, in social media, in our relationships, or in our leaders, it's often difficult to discern the lies from the truth. Areas that were once black and white have now blended into all sorts of grey shades. In search for genuine truth, let's look no further than the God of Truth (Jehovah El Emeth).

Trust originates from God. He is the truth. His Word is truth; therefore, let's dive deeper into the Bible if we hope to know more of the truth and gain wisdom and discernment. How do we do this?

Here are three ways we can spend more time in the Bible and gain spiritual truth:

1. Taste and See Method. As you read a passage or chapter, reflect on it by asking, "What did it mean then? What does it mean now? What does it mean to me personally?"

2. Seek and Find Method. Go to the concordance in the back of your Bible and look up a word such as "adoration." Then, read each verse on the topic of adoration.

3. Mix and Match Method. When reading a verse, look it up in several translations to better understand what the words convey. Many websites offer free translation searches.[10]

Daily Declaration – *I declare that God is the Lord of truth. I can discern more as I spend time with Him and with the Bible. To become wiser, I will invest more time in Bible study.*

Daily Prayer – *Thank you, God, for the Bible. Would you give me a greater desire to read it, learn it, and study it? I want to love the Bible more and gain more of its truth for my life.*

Daily Action – Consider spending more time in Bible study today. Choose one of the methods listed in the devotion, then study for ten to fifteen minutes. Ask God to give you amazing insights and write what you learn in the space below.

....

....

....

....

....

....

....

....

....

....

....

....

....

....

God Hears You

Daily Verse – *During that long period, the king of Egypt died. The Israelites groaned in their slavery and cried out, and their cry for help because of their slavery went up to God. God heard their groaning, and he remembered his covenant with Abraham, with Isaac and with Jacob. So God looked on the Israelites and was concerned about them.* —Exodus 2:23-25 (NIV)

I'm the kind of woman who loves to walk, especially with other people. Great exercise and great conversations occur during a good walk. During a recent walk with a friend, though, we were enjoying a conversation when she grew upset with me. She told me I had interrupted her, but I didn't even realize it. I wasn't being a good listener, and she let me know.

How are your listening skills? Are you the kind of friend who asks good questions and sticks around to hear the answers? Or, like me, do you often become impatient and talk over your friends or interrupt them in your excitement to share? Listening is a gift, an art, and a skill for sure.

Did you know that God is a wonderful listener? In fact, the Bible tells us that He is the God who hears. When we pray, He bends down to listen and pays great attention. Your heavenly Father loves you and wants to hear from you. With compassion, He invites you to share your heart. No lectures. No interruptions. No judgment. Only grace.

Daily Declaration – *I declare that my God loves to hear from me. He pays attention when I talk and enjoys the sound of my voice. Even if He has heard my story before, He will not grow weary with me. I can talk to my God.*

Daily Prayer – *Thank you for being Elohim Shama, the God who hears. Even when no one else listens, you are always available. Help me to remember this and to talk with you more often.*

Daily Action – If God is such an awesome listener, it seems logical that we should want to talk with Him more. Without measuring your words, write a prayer in the space below. Share your heart and know that He loves to hear from you!

The Lord is Your Banner of Victory

Daily Verse – *Moses built an altar and called it The LORD is my Banner. He said, "Because hands were lifted up against the throne of the LORD,' the LORD will be at war against the Amalekites from generation to generation." —Exodus 17:15-16 (NIV)*

I grew up in a large church that had an equally large music program. Among the many choirs, orchestras, and bands was a banner ministry. A group of women hand-made beautiful flags attached to metal poles, and these women paraded the flags around our church. Some flags hung from the ceiling, others were placed at the front of the church, and many were used during praise and worship services.

Banners are used all around us. Colleges use them. Teams use them. Offices use them. The Olympics uses them. A banner that's decorated with team colors and the team mascot will often elicit great devotion and allegiance.

Spiritually speaking, a banner is a symbol of God's presence. It symbolizes the full weight of heaven behind us, in front of us, over us, and beneath us. God tells us that He is a banner over us, and that He protects us, gives us victory, and defeats our enemies. It's because of God's banner of love shielding us that we can walk with peace and confidence.

Daily Declaration – *I declare that God's banner over me is love. He is my Victor and my Champion. I declare that I have the victory in my life today because God is behind me, before me, and all around me.*

Daily Prayer – *Father, thank you for being my Banner, Jehovah Nissi. Your protection is like a memorial over me. I pledge my allegiance to you today and trust you to take care of me.*

Daily Action – If you asked your friends and family, what banner would they say is flying over your life? Would they say that God's banner is raised high? Do they see God at work in your life? If so, describe what you think this looks like. If not, how would you like to raise God's banner higher in your life?

The God Who Loves

Daily Verse – *Long ago the LORD said to Israel: "I have loved you, my people, with an everlasting love. With unfailing love, I have drawn you to myself." —Jeremiah 31:3 (NLT)*

When you think about who loves you the most in your life, who comes to mind? Your mom? Dad? A brother or sister? Grandparent? Cousin? Best friend? Boyfriend? What is it that makes you feel loved by this person?

Personally, I would say that my husband loves me the most of anyone in my life. Yes, my kids, friends, and family members love me too. But my husband is the most consistent, kind, and loving. When others are too busy, he is available. Day after day, he shows up for me. These things make me feel valued, special, and cherished.

Did you know that God loves us and wants us to feel valued, special, and cherished?

Think about a few facets of His love toward us:

- God loves us without any conditions or exceptions (1 Cor. 13).
- Nothing can ever separate us from God's love (Rom. 8:38-39).
- His love never fails (Ps. 36:5-7).
- Nothing we do can make Him love us less (Eph. 2:4-5).
- His love calms us and gives us peace (Zeph. 3:17).

Daily Declaration – *I declare that God loves me. Completely, unconditionally, and without wavering, God deeply loves me. I declare also that God wants what is best for me and for my life. In His love, I can rest.*

Daily Prayer – *Thank you for your love, Lord. I praise you for being Elohim, Ahavah, the God who loves. Because of your love, I am changed. No matter how anyone else behaves or misbehaves, I can find great security in your love.*

Daily Action – Look back over some of the facets of God's love that I shared today. Which of these do you appreciate the most? Why? Take a few moments and thank God for the way he loves you. You may want to write out a prayer of thanksgiving in the space below.

God, the Gardener

Daily Verse – *I am the true vine, and my Father is the gardener. He cuts off every branch in me that bears no fruit, while every branch that does bear fruit, he prunes so that it will be even more fruitful.* —John 15:1-2 (NIV)

Last summer, my husband and I decided to try our hand at herb gardening. We visited Lowe's and picked up a variety of herbs to plant: mint, basil, cilantro, dill, and a few others. Then, we bought large planting pots and dirt to build a container garden. In our garden, we do the work, and the herbs just grow. We water, pull weeds, tend the soil, and put out the bug killer. The herbs' only job is to bloom and become wonderful seasonings.

Have you ever thought about how God is an amazing Gardener? He is referred to in this manner multiple times in the Bible. If God is the Master Gardener, then we must be the beautiful plants in His garden. God plants us, waters us, tills the soil around us, pulls the weeds, sends the sunshine and rain, and cares for all that pertains to our garden.

What is our job then? We must surrender to our Gardener and grow. We aren't supposed to worry about the other plants or the soil or the water. We are to bloom and become wonderful seasonings. Our job is to stay planted and allow God to do His work. His job is everything else.

Daily Declaration – *I declare that God is a master Gardener. He is well able to handle watering, fertilizing, and caring for my garden. I can trust Him to take care of me. I will surrender and allow Him to do the work He needs to do in, with, and through my life.*

Daily Prayer – *Father, I will trust you to be an amazing Gardener in my life. You know how much water and sunlight I need, and you know when to cut back my leaves and branches. I praise you that you are brilliant at taking care of all my concerns.*

Daily Action – How is the garden where you are planted right now? Is it easy to bloom where you are? Or is it hard? In the space below, describe your garden. What makes it a wonderful place and what makes it challenging? How are you growing? What are you learning?

The Lord is Your Redeemer

Daily Verse – *Then all mankind will know that I, the LORD, am your Savior, your Redeemer, the Mighty One of Jacob.* —Isaiah 49:26b (NIV)

Her name was Daisy. She was the cutest, fluffiest, white and gold puffball that we adopted from a local rescue center. Full of energy, happy, and fast as lightning, this dog loved to be outside. One day, she wandered away from our yard. We looked everywhere for her. After hours of searching, we received a call from the pound. Daisy had been spotted running with some wild dogs. The officials at the pound rescued her and gave us a call.

As my husband and I entered the pound, we quickly noticed a terrible stench. Dogs barked like crazy. About halfway down one of the aisles of cages, we spotted out beautiful girl. Her fur was matted, she was completely dirty, and she hung her head in shame. But as we called her name, she looked up, and her face brightened at the sight of us. After paying the pound fees, we took that precious girl home, gave her a bath and far too many hugs. She then ran around the yard, basking in her freedom.

It was a good day—the day that Daisy was redeemed from the pound.

Redeemed. To be redeemed is to be purchased, bought back, paid for, and set free. That's what God has done for us. By sending Jesus, He set us free! And He continues to offer us redemption and freedom … over sin, temptation, depression, doubt, resentment, sexual sin, or whatever binds us and cages us. God redeems all things!

Daily Declaration – *I declare that God is my Redeemer. He is my Jehovah Goes Lakh. Because of Jesus, I can live unbound and free. He paid the price so that I might walk uncaged and unbound.*

Daily Prayer – *Father, thank you for releasing me from my bondage and everything that once kept me caged. Thank you for washing me off, pulling me into your embrace, and setting me free to run and enjoy life. I'm so thankful to be redeemed!*

Daily Action – What do you need God to redeem in your life? Have you become enslaved to anything? Are you stuck? Have you given any ground to the devil? Have you lost territory in areas where you used to live in victory? Take time to pray about these things. You might write out your prayer in the space below. God can redeem anything! He desires for you to live in total freedom!

Your Husband

Daily Verse – *"In that day," declares the LORD, "you will call me 'my husband'; you will no longer call me 'my master.' … I will betroth you to me forever; I will betroth you in righteousness and justice, in love and compassion. I will betroth you in faithfulness, and you will acknowledge the LORD."*
—Hosea 2:16, 19-20 (NIV)

Just yesterday, my husband and I received yet another wedding invitation. I don't think a week has gone by this season when we *didn't* receive an invite to a bridal shower or a wedding. It's just that time of year. And I love weddings… the flowers, the music, the food, the joy, the wedding party. It's a happy day of celebration for everyone.

Honestly, my favorite thing to do at a wedding is to watch the face of the groom as the bride enters the room. While everyone else may be admiring her dress, flowers, hair, and beauty, I like to turn and look at the reaction of the groom. Is he smiling, crying, intently looking at her? Is the groom madly in love with this precious girl he has chosen?

It's interesting to remember that God is our husband. The Bible tells us that we don't need to call Him "Master." Instead, He is our faithful, loving, and compassionate husband. He wants to make us His own—totally and completely. To God, you are His beloved. You are desired, adored, and beautiful. And as you daily "walk down the aisle" toward your heavenly husband, He is beyond pleased with you and delighted that He chose you—and that you accepted His betrothal.

Daily Declaration – *I declare that God is my husband. He has chosen me to be His wife. God will never fail me, cheat on me, or divorce me. I declare that God will always choose me, protect me, love me, and provide for me. I can trust my Heavenly husband!*

Daily Prayer – *Thank you for this beautiful picture of love, Lord. You love me. Thank you for this truth!*

Daily Action – Are you the kind of person who loves weddings? What is the most beautiful wedding you have ever attended? Have you thought about how God is your heavenly husband? How does this name of God encourage you? Complete this sentence: Knowing that God has chosen me to be His makes me feel…

....

....

....

....

....

....

....

....

....

....

....

....

He is Near

Daily Verse – *"Am I not a God near at hand"— GOD's Decree—"and not a God far off? Can anyone hide out in a corner where I can't see him?" GOD's Decree. "Am I not present everywhere, whether seen or unseen?" GOD's Decree.* —Jeremiah 23:23 (MSG)

It's a thing. A real thing. Day or night, my family's dog, Koda, hangs close to us. He's not a lap dog or a snuggly critter, but he does like to be nearby. Near the bathroom door, near the dinner table, near the couch, near the bed, near the shower door. Close proximity is his thing. It's hard to get away from this dog.

Did you know that we serve a God who always sticks nearby, too? The Bible tells us that He is Elohei Mikkrov, the God who is near. There is no getting away from our God. He is there. His presence is close. God will never abandon us.

Truly, He is present everywhere, even though we can't see Him. He is always by our side.

As you deal with the challenges of life, you can count on God to walk along beside you. If your friends are unkind, your parents don't understand, or you feel like your classes are killing you right now, God is with you. As you face life's ups and downs, doubts, sadness, anxiety, fear, insecurity, and hurt feelings, your God sees. He hears, cares, and holds you close. You never need to walk alone; God is always near.

Daily Declaration – *I declare that you are nearby. You never leave me, forsake me, or abandon me to walk alone. I declare that you are by my side—every single second of every single day!*

Daily Prayer – *Thank you, Lord, for staying close. I'm grateful for the nearness of your presence and that you are always with me.*

Daily Action – Do you ever think about how God is always with you and walks beside you? How does it make you feel to know that He is near? How have you experienced and enjoyed His nearness? In the space below, brainstorm a few ways you could enjoy more of His presence today.

....

....

....

....

....

....

....

....

....

....

....

....

....

The Lord, Our Defense

Daily Verse – *Indeed, our shield belongs to the LORD, our king to the Holy One of Israel.* —Psalm 89:18 (NIV)

A woman named Sally was in a terrible custody battle over her two-year-old son. Having little money and few friends, Sally was desperate. When she turned to me, I called a lawyer friend and asked for his help. He willingly agreed to step in at no cost and advocate on behalf of Sally. Even though he had never met her before, he graciously helped Sally gain full custody of her little boy. She was beyond relieved and grateful for his help.

Just like Sally, we often find ourselves in need of representation. We may need a defender in our lives to step in and fight for us. That is what our God is and what He does. He is our Defense, Jehovah Maginnenu. No matter the situation, issue, or challenge, God stands ready to help us.

Consider a few of the ways that God defends us:

- Against false accusations and claims
- From harm and hurt
- Against those who come against us
- Against the devil and his demons
- Against lies that threaten to undo us
- From our own imaginations and incriminations against ourselves

Daily Declaration – *I declare that you are my Defense. You are my amazing Advocate, Attorney, and Defender. You step in and step up for me. I never need to fight alone because you are there to fight with me and for me.*

Daily Prayer – *Father, I'm so grateful to have you as my Defender. You are my Shield, my Protection in battle. Thank you for this truth!*

Daily Action – How do you need God to be your defense today? At work or in class? With a friend or family member? In a challenging situation or in your own thought life? With a temptation or maybe a tangible enemy? God is ready and willing to step in and advocate for you. Take time to discuss your situation with Him. You may want to journal about it below.

7 Truths about Your Heavenly Father

Daily Verse—A father to the fatherless, a defender of widows, is God in his holy dwelling.—Psalm 68:5 (NIV)

When I asked a group of young women to describe their fathers, I received a variety of responses. One girl said her dad was stiff and aloof. Another described her father as being busy and unavailable. Fortunately, some of the girls shared positive traits about their dads. Some of the adjectives used were funny, silly, happy, and kind.

As you think about your own earthly father, what words come to mind? Is he busy and aloof, or is he involved in your life?

No matter what type of earthly dad you have, you also have an amazing heavenly Father. He is your Abba, your Daddy. And this Father is good, reliable, available, and faithful.

In fact, let's look at a few of the traits the Bible uses to describe Him:

1. Your heavenly Father is yours and you are his (Psalm 89:26).
2. You can talk to your Abba at any time (Matthew 6:9).
3. He is always gracious and kind (Romans 8:15).
4. Your heavenly Father adores you (1 John 3:1).
5. Your Abba cares about you deeply. (1 Peter 5:7).
6. He loves to spend time with you (Ephesians 3:12).
7. He is a good Father (Matthew 7:9-11).

Daily Declaration – *I declare that my heavenly Father is good. He is kind, loving, and faithful. No matter how my earthly father has behaved, I can always trust in and depend upon my Abba.*

Daily Prayer – *Thank you, Abba, for being so amazing! Thank you for loving me just as I am and for accepting me completely. I am blessed to have a Father like you.*

Daily Action – Review the descriptions of your heavenly Father, and check out some of those verses. Which of these traits do you most appreciate right now and why? Take a moment to write a prayer to your Abba in the space below.

The Everlasting and Eternal God

Daily Verse – *After the treaty had been made at Beersheba, Abimelek and Phicol the commander of his forces returned to the land of the Philistines. Abraham planted a tamarisk tree in Beersheba, and there he called on the name of the LORD, the Eternal God.* —Genesis 21:32-33 (NIV)

I've been alive for a long time now—long enough to remember a time before computers and cell phones. My grandparents lived before we had television and air conditioning. Their parents lived before we had cars or running water. Time is a funny and strange dynamic, don't you think?

We can get so caught up and worried about one moment, one hour, one week, one month, or even one year. But it all passes so quickly, and just like that, time has moved on. Those moments, hours, weeks, months, and even years have vanished.

When God looks at time, He sees things differently than I do. He is eternal, everlasting, always, and never-ending. Our God has always been, and He will always be. It's completely fascinating and a little hard to wrap my mind around.

This means we can place our trust completely in God because He sits *outside* of time. The universe is a small pebble in the hands of the Creator. God can see the beginning from the end and the end from the beginning. Because of this, we can look to Him for wisdom and guidance.

Daily Declaration – *I declare that God is eternal. He is El Olam, the one who created time and rules over it. I can trust Him with today, tomorrow, next year, and my entire future.*

Daily Prayer – *Lord, thank you for being in control of time. You rule over the past, the present, and the future. Help me to trust you more with my time.*

Daily Action – Because our minds and lives are finite, it can be hard to completely grasp the way God sees time and space. But we do know that God is in control, and He is able to take great care of us. So, what are some things you need to give Him today? What matters are weighing you down? What is stealing your joy and giving you anxiety? Talk to your El Olam about these things.

The Lord of Hosts

Daily Verse – *David said to the Philistine, "You come against me with sword and spear and javelin, but I come against you in the name of the LORD Almighty, the God of the armies of Israel, whom you have defied. This day the LORD will deliver you into my hands, and I'll strike you down and cut off your head. This very day I will give the carcasses of the Philistine army to the birds and the wild animals, and the whole world will know that there is a God in Israel."* —1 Samuel 17:45-46 (NIV)

This is one of my favorite scenes in the Bible. As David faces off against the massive warrior, Goliath, he calls out courageously that he fights in the name of the Lord. Without any timidity or trepidation, young David steps into battle with a cruel and overbearing enemy. And God gives David the victory! David wins. Israel wins. God wins.

Incidentally, the name that David used to describe God in this battle is the Lord of Hosts (Jehovah Tsebaoth Tsaba). The Lord of Hosts is a title of great power. By using this title, David declares that this God is over all angels, as well as the sun, moon, stars, sky, rivers, mountains, the weather, and all people and animals. None is greater than the Lord of Hosts.

My family used to live out in the country when my children were young. One night, we went out, laid on the trampoline, and gazed at the stars. The cloudless sky revealed countless diamonds in the sky, and we couldn't help but stare in awe. As we lay there in the dark, one of my kids said, "Wow! God made all of this, and He keeps them up there and keeps them shining!"

Daily Declaration – *I declare that you are the Lord of Hosts. You are over all things and in control of everything. You made it all and you keep it going.*

Daily Prayer – *Thank you for being the Lord of Hosts! You are an incredible and powerful God. Just like you helped David, you can give me the victory in my life as well.*

Daily Action – What battles are you facing? Are there any Goliaths in your path? Maybe a person, a financial situation, a health issue, or an internal battle you are fighting? Ask the Lord of Hosts to help you and invite Him to display His power in your life and in this battle. Consider journaling about these things below.

He's a Mighty God

Daily Verse – *"Job, are you listening? Have you noticed all this? Stop in your tracks! Take in God's miracle-wonders! Do you have any idea how God does it all, how he makes bright lightning from dark storms? How he piles up the cumulus clouds—all these miracle-wonders of a perfect Mind?" ... "Mighty God! Far beyond our reach! Unsurpassable in power and justice! It's unthinkable that he'd treat anyone unfairly. So, bow to him in deep reverence, one and all! If you're wise, you'll most certainly worship him."* —Job 37:14-16, 23-24 (MSG)

If you met my son, you would probably agree that he is one of the politest young men you have ever met. He is just the consummate nice guy. Beyond that, he is strong. And I often forget this—that is, until I need him to carry or move something heavy. What feels difficult for me is no problem for him.

Similarly, we serve a God who is kind and compassionate. He's good and gentle with us. But He is also strong and powerful. He is mighty, and we often forget about this.

Consider some of the descriptions in today's verses. God creates lighting and makes it shine through the dark storms. Our God piles up cumulus clouds. He is unsurpassable in power and justice, and He treats us with the perfect amount of grace and mercy. Our mighty God is worthy of our worship.

Daily Declaration – *I declare that you are the Mighty God. You still do great miracles, and you control the weather, the clouds, the lightning, and the storms. I will bow in reverence and honor to you.*

Daily Prayer – *Wow, God. You are awesome. When I forget or take you for granted, remind me of your strength. I really do want to worship you!*

Daily Action – Let's take time today to worship our Mighty God! In the space below, make a list of eight to ten ways you have seen God's power displayed over the weather, over the elements, in your life, and in the lives of others. Then, praise God for each of these things. He is worthy of our honor and our worship.

....

....

....

....

....

....

....

....

....

....

....

....

....

Overflowing Fountains

Daily Verse – *For my people have done two evil things: They have abandoned me—the fountain of living water. And they have dug for themselves cracked cisterns that can hold no water at all!* —Jeremiah 2:13 (NLT)

Do you love fountains as much as I do? There is something so beautiful about cascading waters, the slight splash, and the unique aspects of these water features. Whether it's the Fountain of Nations at Disney's Epcot Center in Florida, Bethesda Fountain in Central Park in New York, or the Buckingham Fountain in Chicago—the gorgeous marble statues and artistic creativity never fail to amaze me.

Wedding proposals are often made at fountains. Television shows and movies are filmed in and around fountains. In some places, children splash and play in fountains. They seem to be life-giving, stress-relieving, and refreshing.

The Bible tells us that God is our fountain. In fact, He is called the Fountain of Living Waters. This means that God pours a constant and endless supply of refreshment on us. He fills us, revives us, and offers living water for our thirsty souls. We can sit by His fountain, splash in His waters, enjoy His artistry, and be restored and revived—every single day.

Daily Declaration – *I declare that you are my Fountain of Living Waters, my Maqowr Chay Mayim. In you, I find restoration, renewal, and refreshment. As I sit on the benches near your fountain or splash in its waters, I find hope.*

Daily Prayer – *Lord, help me to come to your fountain more often. I sometimes become tempted to look to other places to receive renewal. But I want to turn to your living waters more often. Help me to do this.*

Daily Action – Where do you find refreshment and renewal during times of drought? Do you turn to a friend, an activity, entertainment, or social media? How might the waters of God's fountain quench your thirst and satisfy your soul more fully? What could you gain by spending more time at His fountain?

A Creative Creator

Daily Verse – *Then God said, "Let the land produce vegetation: seed-bearing plants and trees on the land that bear fruit with seed in it, according to their various kinds." And it was so.* —Genesis 1:11 (NIV)

Have you ever taken one of those aptitude tests to discover areas you are gifted in? Perhaps you found out you are strong in verbal reasoning or mathematical reasoning. Your test may reveal that you have strong skills in judgment and reasoning, data interpretation, or people skills.

When my daughter was given an aptitude test in high school, she scored at the top of the charts in design skills. The test suggested that she was incredibly gifted in the elements and practice of design, arrangement, composition, and conceptualization. All these years later, it's not surprising that my girl is a successful fashion designer, model, and social media coordinator. God created her to be uniquely creative in her own special way.

God created you to be uniquely creative in your own special way as well. You have gifts, inclinations, talents, and abilities that make you the only person on this planet who is just like you. God specially crafted you this way. You are the only individual in the world that can accomplish what He has created you to accomplish. No one else can do you, contribute as you, or impact others as you will do. So, don't be afraid to be yourself! Be the woman God designed you to be.

Daily Declaration – *I declare that my God is the Creator of all things. God is Elohim, who created me as an exceptional and extraordinary woman with a purpose. God made my life to matter, to make a difference, and to contribute great things that can benefit and serve others.*

Daily Prayer – *Father, would you remind me of how important I am to you and to this world? Thank you for creating me and for making me special. Bolster my courage to do what you have created me to do in this life.*

Daily Action – How can you use your gifts and talents to make a difference? How might God use your life to impact and help other people? Make a list of three ways you feel you can add value to this world. After making the list, pray over each of these areas and invite God to open doors for you to use these gifts.

Kings and Kingdoms

Daily Verse – *Who should not fear you, King of the nations? This is your due. Among all the wise leaders of the nations and in all their kingdoms, there is no one like you.* —Jeremiah 10:7 (NIV)

Have you ever noticed how many shows and movies are about kings, queens, monarchs, and royalty these days? We seem to be obsessed with the whole notion of kings and their kingdoms.

But this is a not a new phenomenon. In Bible days, the people were captivated by the idea of kings and kingdoms as well. Perhaps that is why there is so much mention of these topics, especially in the Old Testament.

Of all the kings mentioned in the Bible, there is one that stands above them all—and that is God, the King of the nations. He rules and reigns with power and honor. He is Melek HaGovim, and there is no one else like Him. Other kings and kingdoms come and go, but our King rules for all of eternity.

Because God is King, there is no panic in heaven—ever. Our God controls all things at all times. Pastor Adrian Rogers puts it this way: "God has never stepped down from His throne." [11]

Daily Declaration – *I declare that my God is the King. He is King of all nations and is in complete control of all things. Others may come and go, but my God is always on His throne.*

Daily Prayer – *Lord, would you help me remember that you are always in charge? No matter how much chaos and craziness happens around me on this earth, you are still King over all the nations.*

Daily Action – What difference does it make that God is the King of all nations? How does this impact your life, your worries, your challenges, and your future? In the space below, complete this sentence: Because God is on His throne as the King, I...

He is the Living God

Daily Verse – *As the deer pants for streams of water, so my soul pants for you, my God. My soul thirsts for God, for the living God. When can I go and meet with God?* —Psalm 42:1-2 (NIV)

Years ago, the Coca-Cola Company used a slogan that everyone attributed to their brand. They would claim, "Coke, it's the REAL THING." Pepsi wasn't the real thing, RC Cola wasn't the real thing, store-brand soft drinks weren't real. Only Coke was the real cola. For years, we all thought of Coca-Cola in this manner.

In the Bible days, people worshipped many gods, idols, and objects. They worshipped other people, creation, and gods made from melted gold. There were a myriad of false gods in those days. To prevent confusion, our God was called the Living God, El Chay. The other gods were not alive; they were dead or inanimate, unable to perform any miracles whatsoever.

But our God is alive! He can actually save people, perform miracles, and make a difference in the lives of His children.

Today, we, too, are tempted to worship idols. We look to people, programs, politicians, and even pastors to save us. But none of these things or people can measure up to God and His greatness. Only the real God, the One true God, the Living God, deserves our praise and adoration. We can meet with Him every single day—and He can actually solve our dilemmas and fix our issues.

Daily Declaration – *I declare that God is the Living God. He is El Chay, alive and worthy of my worship. My God is able to perform miracles and handle my problems. He's not overwhelmed or aloof; instead, He stands ready and willing to help.*

Daily Prayer – *Father, remind me to turn to you for all my needs. Other people are great, but only you are the Living God, the powerful miracle-worker. I want to worship you alone as God!*

Daily Action – What, or who, is on your heart today? A friend? A family member? A co-worker or roommate? Write a prayer to the Lord and share your concerns. Then invite Him to powerfully work in each situation.

Consuming Fire

Daily Verse – *So be careful not to break the covenant the LORD your God has made with you. Do not make idols of any shape or form, for the LORD your God has forbidden this. The LORD your God is a devouring fire; he is a jealous God.* —Deuteronomy 4:23-24 (NLT)

I was watching one of those home renovation shows recently and saw one of the hosts do the most unusual thing. She was trying to get rid of some remnants left in the wall from old wallpaper. Rather than using a knife or scissors to cut off the scraps, she instead took a small blowtorch and burned off the fragments. The fire did the work powerfully, efficiently, and quickly.

Fire. It's a powerful substance that we use for a variety of purposes. Fire warms us. Fire destroys leaves and brush. Fire can be used to light candles and lanterns. And God calls Himself a Consuming Fire, Akal Esha. It's an unusual term. In simple terms, our God wants our hearts.

More than anything, God wants us to love Him and to be close to Him. God will use His fire to burn away anything that keeps us at a distance. With this fire, He purifies, transforms, heals, and transforms us into the image of His Son. This process is not always pleasant, but the fire works powerfully, quickly, and efficiently in our lives. And when the fire has done its work, we will look a little more like Jesus.

Daily Declaration – *I declare that God is a Consuming Fire. He knows what needs to be burned away in my life. I will trust God to purify, cleanse, and transform me. He is the master renovator and remodeler in my life.*

Daily Prayer – *Father, to be consumed by your fire is not always easy, but I do want to be close to you. I want to know you more and to love you more. So I give you permission to keep working in my life. My "yes" is on the table.*

Daily Action – Honesty time: What do you need to let God burn away in your life? Are there old scraps of wallpaper hanging on the walls of your life that need to be removed? Are there habits, relationships, thoughts, music you listen to, or shows you watch that God may want to remove? Why not spend time talking about this with Him today? If you aren't ready to let go quite yet, talk to God about why you are holding on so tightly to something or someone.

The Only Wise God

Daily Verse – *To the only wise God be glory forever through Jesus Christ! Amen.* —Romans 16:27 (NIV)

Do you ever find yourself in need of wisdom—such as when you're deciding on classes to take for the semester? Or whether to date that guy or take a certain job? In life—especially in the early adult years—there are several big decisions that need to be made. These decisions require wisdom.

Did you know that God is called the Only Wise God? He is Theos Monos Sophos, and He is able to give you His perspective on things. We can press in close to Him and gain insights for our lives.

When we take our decisions to God, pray, read the Bible, and talk with wise counselors, God will impart onto us both wisdom and understanding. So, where would you like to begin? What do you need to discuss with your Father?

Daily Declaration – *I declare that God is the Only Wise God. He is Theos Monos Sophos, and I can trust in His wisdom. I will go to Him, talk to Him, and learn from Him more often.*

Daily Prayer – *Lord, since you are the Only Wise God, I want to seek you quicker and more often. Remind me that you are wiser than any of my friends, mentors, family members, or counselors.*

Daily Action – God promises to give us His wisdom. In what areas do you need that wisdom today? Write a few decisions you are praying over right now. Then, talk them over with the Lord and invite Him to give you greater insight and understanding on how to proceed. Ask God to clearly show you the next steps.

The Lord, My Sanctifier

Daily Verse – *Then the LORD said to Moses, "Say to the Israelites, 'You must observe my Sabbaths. This will be a sign between me and you for the generations to come, so you may know that I am the LORD, who makes you holy.'"* —Exodus 31:12-13 (NIV)

Every Tuesday and Thursday, a woman named Louise would come to my family's house to clean. She had an amazing way of making the house look, smell, and feel crisp and clean. The bathrooms, the bedding, the clothes, and the entire atmosphere of the house felt refreshed because of this wonderful lady.

In a similar fashion, our God is known for His powerful ability to clean and refresh. He is called the Lord my Sanctifier. That's what sanctification means—to cleanse, set apart, restore, renew, and refresh. In the Old Testament, sanctification involved fires, altars, blood, and animal sacrifices. However, thanks to Jesus' death on the cross, sanctification is simpler for us to receive as New Testament believers.

It's not rocket science. We draw close to Jesus and remain by His side. Jesus does the rest. He cleanses, renews, restores, and refreshes our lives. We don't need to go into hours and hours of morbid introspection. We just need to spend time with God and allow Him to take care of the cleansing work. Our part is to surrender. His part is to sanctify.

Daily Declaration – *I declare that God is my Sanctifier. He is Lord, and He can perform a cleansing, restorative work in my life every day. I will surrender to Him and allow Him to have His way.*

Daily Prayer – *Father, I submit to you as my Lord and Savior. I surrender and invite you to cleanse me, heal me, and renew me. Still my heart and give me the faith to trust you with all of this work.*

Daily Action – What work is God doing in your life? Where is He cleansing, renewing, restoring, stretching, and sanctifying you? How is He making you more like Jesus? Take a few moments and write about these things in the space below.

Mighty in Battle

Daily Verse – *Then the LORD said to Moses, "Say to the Israelites, 'You must observe my Sabbaths. This will be a sign between me and you for the generations to come, so you may know that I am the LORD, who makes you holy.'"* —Exodus 31:12-13 (NIV)

Mary is a close friend of mine. Everyone seems to love her because of how encouraging, friendly, kind, and hilarious she is. But most people are unaware that Mary struggles with anxiety and depression. These issues have plagued her for years, and she fights daily battles with these mental health challenges. Although some days are better than others, Mary believes this fight will continue, at least to some degree, for the rest of her life.

Are you fighting a battle today? Maybe you struggle with anxiety, depression, or fear like my friend Mary. Perhaps you fight against insecurity or self-doubt. Or it could be that your battle is physical, like an addiction. You may struggle to win over drug or alcohol addiction, a sexual addiction, a food addiction, or something else.

Every one of us fights battles. I don't know anyone who doesn't struggle with something. You may not see it, sense it, or know about it. But everyone is fighting something.

That's where God comes in. He is Jehovah, Mighty in Battle. Whatever battle you are facing, the Lord promises to be strong and mighty. He will fight for you and with you. God is in your corner, and He will empower you! Invite Him to show Himself strong on your behalf today.

Daily Declaration – *I declare that my God is Jehovah Gibbor Milchamah, the Lord Mighty in Battle. He will fight with me and for me. I declare that I can stand strong today because He is beside me.*

Daily Prayer – *Thank you for being the Lord Mighty in Battle. Thank you for fighting with me and for me. I ask for your tremendous power to give me victory today!*

Daily Action – Where do you need God's help today? You don't have to fight alone! Take time to write a prayer about some of the battles you are facing. Invite God to step into your situation and give you a breakthrough of hope.

God is Judge

Daily Verse – *Far be it from you to do such a thing—to kill the righteous with the wicked, treating the righteous and the wicked alike. Far be it from you! Will not the Judge of all the earth do right?* —Genesis 18:25 (NIV)

If you turned on your television right now, you could probably find a show featuring a courtroom and a judge. On reality television, documentaries, the news, and regular programming, we see judges who make rulings in courts. Defendants, plaintiffs, and their lawyers stand before a judge and learn their fate. It's how our justice system is constructed.

Similarly, throughout the Bible we find judges, justice systems, and court proceedings. Popular judges in the Bible include Samson, Deborah, and Gideon. Judges have a powerful position.

They rule. They deliver. They save. They guide. Even more, they determine and decide—for this reason, they are respected, trusted, and feared.

Have you thought about how God is a judge? In fact, His name Shamhat means God is Judge. God is the ultimate judge. He will always do what is best and what is right. Nothing misses His notice or slips past His sight. No one fools Him or pulls one over on God. He may delay His judgment, but He will have the final say. Our God is sovereign over all the earth. He sits on His throne and always remains alert.

Daily Declaration – *I declare that my God is the ultimate judge. He will judge the Earth and have the final say. I can trust God to handle all matters well and in His perfect timing.*

Daily Prayer – *Father, encourage my heart when it grows weak and when I witness evil winning. I want to trust you to step in and judge fairly—even when I can't see or hear you. You are the great Judge who is worthy of all my respect and trust.*

Daily Action – What do you need God to judge or make right in your life today? Is there a situation, an injustice, or a place that needs justice? I encourage you to invite God to step in and make things right. Ask Him to give you extra peace and grace as you wait for Him to judge.

The God of All Comfort

Daily Verse – *All praise to the God and Father of our Master, Jesus the Messiah! Father of all mercy! God of all healing counsel! He comes alongside us when we go through hard times, and before you know it, he brings us alongside someone else who is going through hard times so that we can be there for that person just as God was there for us. We have plenty of hard times that come from following the Messiah, but no more so than the good times of his healing comfort—we get a full measure of that, too.* —2 Corinthians 1:3-5 (MSG)

My bed's comforter is large and white, and it's extremely soft, comfortable, and cozy. I love climbing into bed at night and snuggling beneath it. Maybe you, too, have soft bedding like this as well.

The word "comfort" means to be cheered and consoled—to have your hurt or distressed feelings eased. God is a Comforter to us. In fact, He is called the God of All Comforts, Theos Pas Paraklesis.

This means that our God can comfort us deeply and meaningfully. His comfort is lasting and real. It's tempting to find temporary comfort in food, drink, clothes, people, activity, and success, but none of these things offer lasting comfort. Real, deep, and sustaining comfort is only found in the Lord of All Comfort.

Daily Declaration – *I declare that God is the God of All Comfort. He will come alongside me and take me through any situation. I am then able to comfort others just as I was comforted.*

Daily Prayer – *Father, thank you for being the God of All Comforts. I ask you to deeply comfort me when I am in pain so that I may comfort others as well. I ask that, as you comfort me, you will make me a comforter.*

Daily Action – I've heard it said that God doesn't comfort us to make us comfortable. Instead, He comforts us so we can comfort others. How has God comforted you? How have you offered comfort to those around you? Who might you comfort today? Write a prayer inviting God to use you to provide hope and comfort to at least one person today.

The Lord is With You

Daily Verse – *When the angel of the LORD appeared to Gideon, he said, "The LORD is with you, mighty warrior."* —Judges 6:12 (NIV)

Throughout the Bible, we hear stories about an angel of the Lord showing up and speaking to a particular person about a particular matter. Often, the angel uses these words: "The Lord is with you." These words actually represent a Bible name of God, Jehovah Immeka. This means "The Lord is with you."

God is with both you and me. His strong presence empowers us. Day after day, God walks with us and never leaves us to face life alone. We never need to make this journey on our own. Not for a single moment.

You may not be able to sense God is with you with your physical senses, but He is beside you, nonetheless.

Think about it:
- When you wake up, God is with you.
- As you head out the door, God goes before you.
- As you take an exam, attend a class, or do your job, God is alongside you.
- While hanging out with your friends, God is in the midst.
- As you get ready for bed, He is there.
- When you lay your head on your pillow to sleep, God is right beside you and watching over you.
- God will never leave you.

Daily Declaration – *I declare that God is always with me. He is Jehovah Immeka. I declare that God will never leave me, abandon me, nor forsake me.*

Daily Prayer – *Thank you, Lord, for staying by my side at all times. I'm grateful that I don't have to walk through this life alone. You are always with me! Please remind me of this truth today.*

Daily Action – Here's a fun activity for you today—go on a God hunt. Be on the lookout for reminders of God's nearness. When you read the Bible and a verse jumps out at you, take that as God speaking. When a friend sends a nice text to you or the lyrics to a song deeply minister to your spirit, take that from the Lord. Write a prayer in the space below and invite God to make you more aware of His presence. He is always with you!

The Lord Who Rewards

Daily Verse – *Destroying armies come against Babylon. Her mighty men are captured, and their weapons break in their hands. For the LORD is a God who gives just punishment; he always repays in full.* —Jeremiah 51:56 (NLT)

Have you ever planted anything in the dirt—maybe seeds, small plants, or a container garden? Or perhaps you grew up on a farm?

Two years ago, I purchased several packs of wildflower seeds and threw those seeds all over the bare places in our yard. I didn't do much digging or fertilizing. Instead, I tossed out hundreds of those little seeds and then went on with life. Nothing happened for almost two years.

But just a few weeks ago, hundreds of beautiful marigold wildflowers bloomed. They are gorgeous and cover one area of the garden. The process took longer than I had expected and only one color of flower bloomed, but I truly did reap what I had sowed. The law of the harvest worked itself out in my backyard.

God is a God who allows us to reap what we sow. He is the Lord Who Rewards, Jehovah Gmolah. We can always expect Him to pay in full. He will reward, repay, and send a harvest. So what are we planting? What kinds of seeds are we planting into the ground—good seeds or bad seeds?

Daily Declaration – *I declare that God is the Lord Who Rewards. He always pays in full—both blessing and punishment. I will plant good seeds so that I may be blessed abundantly with good.*

Daily Prayer – *Father, you are the God who allows us to reap what we sow. Would you lead me to plant healthy and positive seeds in my life? Thank you for rewarding and blessing those who seek you.*

Daily Action – God wants to bless you today; however, He is a just God. When we plant anger, jealousy, and gossip, we will reap a harvest of those things. But if we plant kindness, love, grace, and compassion, we will reap a harvest of these character traits instead. What would you like to plant in your garden today? Write or draw a few of the flowers and plants you would like to cultivate in your life today. I challenge you to plan and prepare for an amazing garden!

God is Holy

Daily Verse – *Then Joshua told the people: "You can't do it; you're not able to worship GOD. He is a holy God. He is a jealous God. He won't put up with your fooling around and sinning. When you leave GOD and take up the worship of foreign gods, he'll turn right around and come down on you hard. He'll put an end to you—and after all the good he has done for you!" —Joshua 24:19-20 (MSG)*

Holiness. The church doesn't talk much about this topic today. To be holy is to be devout, deeply devoted, and righteous. To live holy is to live a clean lifestyle. God wants us to be holy because He is holy.

Think about the last time you were covered in sweat. Maybe you were running, playing a sport, working in the yard or in the garden. Whatever the case, there is something refreshing about washing off the filth by taking a hot shower.

Doesn't it feel amazing?

Similarly, we need regular *spiritual* showers. We need to confess our sins to God and allow Him to wash over us with His warm faucets of grace and forgiveness. When He applies spiritual soap, shampoo, and splashing waters of mercy, we are deeply cleansed. Nothing is sweeter than being cleansed by the kindness of our Lord. We were designed to live right with God.

Daily Declaration – *I declare that God is the Holy God. He is Elohim, Kedoshim. I want to live a holy life because God wants this for me. He will enable me to do this as I press close and confess my sins.*

Daily Prayer – *Thank you, Lord, for your mercy and grace. You are kind, gracious, and quick to forgive. If we confess our sins, you are faithful and just to forgive and cleanse us.*

Daily Action – Although our sins could never cause us to lose our relationship with God, we can certainly break our fellowship with Him. Is there anything you need to make right with God today? Maybe you need to confess something that you said, thought, did, or didn't do. Take a few minutes to pray, and then write a prayer asking God to forgive you. He will do so. Then you can arise and live cleansed and refreshed and be right with God once again.

The Lord, My Strength

Daily Verse – *The LORD is my strength and my shield; my heart trusts in him, and he helps me. My heart leaps for joy, and with my song I praise him.* —Psalm 28:7 (NIV)

Are you a woman who is strong? Maybe you lift weights or run miles at a time. Or maybe you're the kind of girl who can always be trusted to remove stubborn lids from jars or lift heavy objects. To be strong is to be capable, durable, robust, and substantial.

Did you know that we can also find our strength in God? He is Jehovah Uzi, The Lord My Strength. His strength empowers us with strength. On days when we are weary, He is strong. When we lack motivation to face the day, God gives us what we need. As life throws heavy challenges our way, we can depend on His strength to get us through.

Consider a few of the unique ways in which our God provides His strength:

- God upholds and helps us (Isaiah 41:10).
- God infuses us with power (Isaiah 40:29).
- The Lord restores and makes us strong, firm, and steadfast (1 Peter 5:10).
- God helps me stand strong when it's hard to stand (Habakkuk 3:19).
- His strength helps me to sing—even on hard mornings (Psalm 59:16).
- His Word strengthens my weary soul (Psalm 119:28).
- When I feel afraid and timid, God strengthens me with power (2 Timothy 1:7).

Daily Declaration – *I declare that God is the Lord my Strength. I can lean on and depend upon Him. In every challenge and in every situation, I can look to Him for help!*

Daily Prayer – *Father, thank you for being my strength. Uphold me, help me, and infuse me with your power today. I need you, Lord.*

Daily Action – Review the list of ways that God proves His strength for us. (You may want to look up these Bible verses as well.) Which one of these speaks to you the most? Where do you need God's strength today? What are the weak areas in your life? Where do you need an infusion of hope? Write about these things in the space below.

....

....

....

....

....

....

....

....

....

....

....

....

....

O Lord, Save Me

Daily Verse – *O Lord, save! May the King answer us when we call.* —Psalm 20:9 (NLV)

Crazy. Chaotic. Unhinged. Weird. These are the words I would use to describe the world in which we live in today. If you haven't noticed already, it's a mess out there. From crazy viruses, violence, and natural disasters, we are living in the strangest of times. For you, as a young adult, this may feel like the norm. You may have never really known anything except for the bizarre status quo that is our world today.

So where do we turn? Where do we search to find hope in the midst of all this?

We can turn to the God who saves, the God who answers us when we call. He is Jehovah Hoshea, and He can rescue us. Our God gives us victory, pulls us out of the messes, rescues us, and provides light in the darkest of days. We can call on Him at any time, for any reason, and from any place.

When you doubt everything, *call on Him.*

When you are in pain, *call on Him.*

As you start to feel afraid, *call on Him.*

When you are struggling, *call on Him.*

As you feel anxious or unsure, *call on Him.*

When the walls close in on you, *call on Him.*

You can always call on your God, the Lord who saves!

Daily Declaration – *I declare that I can always call on you, my God who saves. You are dependable and available, and I know you love me. I will call upon you!*

Daily Prayer – *Father, I want to call upon you more often and for more things. Help me remember that I can always call upon you. You are able to save me!*

Daily Action – What do you need to call on God for today? In the space below, list a few issues, concerns, or worries that have been on your heart lately. Then, give each one to God and ask for His help. He can heal, fix, mend, forgive, help, save, and restore. Why not invite Him to do these things right now?

My Favorite Name of God

Daily Verse – *Good and upright is the LORD; therefore he instructs sinners in his ways.* —Psalm 25:8 (NIV)

A friend recently asked me which of God's names is my favorite, as well as which one I think is the most important. There are many great names for God, but perhaps the most essential one that we need to believe is "The Lord is Good." He is Adonai Tov.

Why does this name matter so much?

Think about it. If God really is good, then we will have no reason to doubt Him. Instead, we will trust Him and believe that He is with us and for us. We will sleep better at night and work harder during the day. If we truly believe that God is good, then our relationships will be sweeter, we will face the future without fear, and we will feel more confident inside our own skin.

If we truly believe that God is good, this will "color" and affect everything else that we believe. It will almost serve like a social media filter for our perspective on life. If I do not believe that God is good, however, then the opposite will happen—everything will fall apart. We will lack joy, peace, and contentment. We will doubt God at every turn and be skeptical about everyone and everything.

So which will it be? Will we spend our lives enjoying God's goodness, or will we live doubtful, cynical lives? The choice is ours.

Daily Declaration – *I declare that my God is good. He is upright and perfect in all His ways. Even when I don't understand, I will choose to trust that He is good.*

Daily Prayer – *Father, help me not to be a skeptic. Instead, make me a woman of great faith, one who trusts in a good God. I want to trust in you more. Please help my unbelief.*

Daily Action – Think about your perspective today. Do you look at God through the filter that says He is good? Or are you more of a skeptic, a doubter, and a critic? As you think about your future, which type of person would you like to be? Talk these things over with God today. He can handle your honesty. Use the space below to write your prayer.

Thank you for taking this journey with me!

It's been a great joy to hang out with you over these past ninety days!

Although our time together is complete in this devotional book, your spiritual growth and devotion to God can continue.

I encourage you to keep praying, reading the Bible, journaling, and trusting that God has amazing plans ahead for your life.

In the meantime, I'd love to connect with you on social media.

You can find me on every major social channel, and on my website.

To visit the website, go to www.melanieredd.com.

You can also shoot me an email at hope@melanieredd.com.

It would be amazing to hear from you!

More Great Resources for You

100 Names of God, Christopher Hudson

All Things Are Possible: A Guided Journal for Christian Women, Melanie Redd

How to Stop Worrying and Start Living Again: Time-Tested Methods for Conquering Worry, Dale Carnegie

Knowing God, J.I. Packer

Praying Through the Names of God, Tony Evans

Sacred Rest: Recover Your Life, Renew Your Energy, Restore Your Sanity, Saundra Dalton-Smith, MD

Stepping Closer to the Savior, Melanie Redd

The Names of God, Ann Spangler

The Names of God, Marilyn Hickey

The Pursuit of God, A.W. Tozer

About the Author

Melanie is an author, blogger, speaker, podcaster, and health coach.

She's been married to Randy for the past thirty years and serves alongside him in ministry. They love to travel, eat great food, play golf and pickleball, and hang out with friends and family.

Additionally, she's mom to two awesome young adults and a crazy Australian shepherd named Koda.

God's grace never ceases to amaze her.

Find out more about Melanie and her ministry at www.melanieredd.com.

Names of God Index

Day 43 – The God Who Meets You

Day 44 – El Nekamoth, God Who Avenges

Day 45 – El Nathan Neqamah, the God Who Avenges Me

Day 46 – El Hayyay, the God of My Life

Day 47 – Elohim Ozer Li, God My Help

Day 48 – Adonai, Master Over All

Day 49 – Adonai, the Lord

Day 50 – God, the One to Whom I Tune My Life

Day 51 – El Shaddai, the Almighty God

Day 52 – Lord, God Almighty

Day 53 – El Simchath Gili, God is My Exceeding Joy

Day 54 – Jehovah Rohi, the Lord is My Shepherd

Day 55 – Jehovah Rohi, the Lord is My Shepherd

Day 56 – Jehovah Ori, the Lord My Light

Day 57 – Gelah Raz, the Revealer of Mysteries

Day 58 – Gelah Raz, the Revealer of Mysteries

Day 59 – Jehovah Rophe, the Lord Our Healer

Day 60 – Miqweh Yisrael, the Hope of Israel

Day 61 – The Lord, My Hope

Day 62 – Jehovah El Emeth, the Lord God of Truth

Day 63 – Elohim Shama, the God Who Hears

Day 64 – Jehovah Nissi, the Lord My Banner

Day 65 – Elohim Ahavah, the God Who Loves

Day 66 – Georgos, the Gardener

Day 67 – Jehovah Goelekh, the Lord, Your Redeemer

Day 68 – Ba'al, the Husband

Day 69 – Elohei Mikkarov, the God Who is Near

Day 70 – Jehovah Maginnenu, the Lord Our Defense

Day 71 – Abba, Our Heavenly Father

Day 72 – Elohenu Olam, the Everlasting God

Day 73 – Elohim Tsebaoth, the God of Hosts

Day 74 – Hode, Majesty

Day 75 – Maqowr Chay Mayim, Fountain of Living Water

Day 76 – Elohim, the Strong Creator God

Day 77 – Eli Maelekhi, Our King

Day 78 – El Chay, the Living God

Day 79 – Esh Oklah, a Consuming Fire

Day 80 – Theos Monos Sophos, the Only Wise God

Day 81 – Jehovah Qadash, the Lord Who Sanctifies

Day 82 – Jehovah Gibbor Milchamah, the Lord, Mighty in Battle

Day 83 – Jehovah Hashpet, the Lord, the Judge

Day 84 – Theos Pas Paraklesis, the God of
All Comfort

Day 85 – Jehovah Immeka, the Lord
is With You

Day 86 – Jehovah El Gemuval, the Lord God
of Recompense

Day 87 – Elohim Kedoshim, the Holy God

Day 88 – Jehovah Uzzi, the Lord My Strength

Day 89 – Jehovah Hoshea, O Lord, Save

Day 90 – Adonai Tov, the Lord is Good

Topic Index

End Notes

1. https://adaa.org/understanding-anxiety/facts-statistics

2. https://www.apa.org/monitor/2013/06/college-students

3. https://www.crosswalk.com/devotionals/desert/streams-in-the-desert-oct-19-1438083.html

4. https://www.goodreads.com/quotes/140315-worry-is-like-a-rocking-chair-it-gives-you-something

5. https://utmost.org/classic/one-of-god%E2%80%99s-great-don%E2%80%99ts-classic/

6. http://repassinc.com/2016/04/4125/#:~:text=A%20social%20experiment%20was%20conducted%20years%20ago.&text=The%20second%20group%20directed%20to,group%20(with%20the%20fence).

7. https://www.foxcarolina.com/news/watch-gigi-graham-speaks-about-her-father/video_a0f025f4-bfcc-5709-90d9-956fbc59f676.html

8. https://www.lyrics.com/lyric-lf/2109449/OCP+Session+Choir/I+Will+Arise+and+Go+to+Jesus

9. https://quotefancy.com/quote/1528031/Adrian-Rogers-God-only-wants-for-us-what-we-would-want-for-ourselves-if-we-were-smart

10. https://www.amazon.com/Stepping-Closer-Savior-Melanie-Redd/dp/1615071385

11. https://www.oneplace.com/ministries/love-worth-finding/read/devotionals/love-worth-finding/love-worth-finding-november-16-2015-11745133.html